The CompleteLandlord.com™

ULTIMATE
PROPERTY
MANAGEMENT
HANDBOOK

The CompleteLandlord.com™

ULTIMATE
PROPERTY
MANAGEMENT
HANDBOOK

William A. Lederer

WILEY

John Wiley & Sons, Inc.

Published by John Wiley & Sons, Inc., Hoboken, New Jersey.
Published simultaneously in Canada.

For general information on our other products and services or for technical support, please contact our
Customer Care Department within the United States at (800) 762-2974, outside the United States at (317)
572-3993 or fax (317) 572-4002.

Wiley also publishes its books in a variety of electronic formats. Some content that appears in print may
not be available in electronic books. For more information about Wiley products, visit our web site at
www.wiley.com.

Library of Congress Cataloging-in-Publication Data

Lederer, William A., 1961–
    The CompleteLandlord.com ultimate property management handbook/by William A. Lederer.
      p. cm.
    Includes index.
    ISBN 978-0-470-32317-5 (pbk.)
      1. Real estate management.   2. Rental housing—Management.   3. Landlord and tenant.   4. Real
    estate investment. I. Title.

HD1394.L43   2009
333.33'8068—dc22   2008045570

Printed in the United States of America.

10 9 8 7 6 5 4 3 2 1

In honor of my family: Renda, Adam, Eric, and Muriel Lederer;

To Jill, John, Robert, Sarah, and Edward Doherty; Peggy, Marc (one of America's great real estate investors and landlords), Josh, Davis, and Chloe Blum;

And in memory of Frederick Lederer, Beverly and Irwin Lippmann, and Stella Natenberg, anyone's idea of a great real estate asset and team member

CONTENTS

ACKNOWLEDGMENTS

I am pleased to acknowledge those without whose help and guidance neither this series nor my landlording odyssey would be complete:

- My copy, editorial, graphics, and marketing team of Bridget McCrea, Shannon Vargo, Linda Indig, Mohammed Ejaz Ali, Brian Neill, Beth Zipko, and Kim Dayman, who really pulled through for me and to whom I am much indebted. A big thank you and recommendation to the best non-fiction literary agent in America and my great friend, Cynthia Zigmund.

- My inspirations: the courageous, selfless and impactful John Wood of Room to Read, business leader and good friend Dean Debiase, and real estate entrepreneur/attorney/friend Dr. Arnold S. Goldstein, Esq.

- My wife Renda and mother Muriel deserve much credit for this ultimate series, our education in landlording, and the staying force to persist. Too seldom do family members get their due in these endeavors. I have been blessed beyond belief.

- My long-time colleagues Enid Becker, Jonas Hedsund, and Jay Rawlings; accountant and lawyers Harry Kramer, Stewart Schechter, Peter Lieberman, and Todd Mazur; and my former colleagues Bruce Masterson, Cindy Fitzgerald, and Paul Barrett.

- Mona Hellinga as my favorite and utterly professional residential real estate agent.

- My friends and business partners at Buildium property management software, including Michael Monteiro and Dimitri Georgakopoulos.

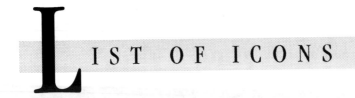

LIST OF ICONS

Money Savers

These sections are designed to save you money. Use the information in them to make frugal decisions regarding your cash outlay when investing in and running your properties.

Money Makers

Here's where you'll learn how to make money in real estate. Ferret out the best possible tips and advice from these sections of the book and you'll be well braced to earn a living and more from your real estate investments.

Time Savers

We know there are only so many hours in a day, so use these areas of the book to shave precious time from your schedule and maximize the time spent on your landlording and real estate investment business.

INTRODUCTION

Whether you came into the property management field intentionally or by accident, you've picked up the right book to help guide you through the ups and downs of your new position.

This book, combined with the real estate investment and landlording books that complete this series, will equip you to take on just about anything that comes your way as a property manager.

This book is designed to serve you, the reader, in several ways. You can read it from cover to cover, stick to those sections that are most applicable to your situation, and/or supplement it with the knowledge that you'll find in the other two volumes. Regardless of how you tackle it, the key is for you to come away with a broad knowledge of exactly what it means to be a successful property manager.

In this book, you'll be on the inside track of property management circles. You'll learn about the skills, aptitude, and attitude of successful property managers; you'll get the best information in achieving scale and setting up systems; and you'll learn the pros and cons of outsourcing the property management function to one or more third parties.

The editorial team at CompleteLandlord.com, publisher of the *Landlord Profit Letter* and numerous special reports, books, and monitors of the CompleteLandlord Forum, has more than 25 years of landlord, property investment, rental management, and overall real estate experience. We also have a dedicated staff of attorneys and advisors who review our articles and forms library to ensure accuracy and compliance with all federal, state, and local real estate laws.

CompleteLandlord.com is for people like you: landlords and property investors. It's the online destination that thousands of savvy landlords and real estate investors go to for real-world advice on managing properties and tenants, as well as to pick up products, services, and essential forms. All our efforts are aimed at helping people run a more profitable and successful real estate business.

We've also assembled an advisory team of more than a dozen landlords from diverse places such as Ohio, Texas, Georgia, and Illinois (just to name a few). This team is not afraid to mix it up and share the real scoop on what it's like to be a landlord. They review and comment on (and sometimes argue about) our product in order to share insights with us (and you) on money and time-saving strategies and tips to help build real wealth with investment properties. The advisory team includes landlords who own, manage, and have sold both large and small multi- and single-family properties, as well as other investment real estate.

Now it's time to start on your own road to successful property management. We'll be here to help, every step of the way, both through the book that you hold in your hands and via our online home, CompleteLandlord.com. We wish you the best of luck with your new business!

About the Product

The CompleteLandlord.com Property Management Solution helps eliminate the excessive burden of paperwork associated with managing rental properties. In contrast to most property management software on the market, Property Management Solution is easy to use, simple to navigate, and it is appropriate for rental property owners with one to one thousand units due to its unique, scalable design. And, since it is an online platform, you can access your rental property information from any Internet location, thereby providing the optimum flexibility for all landlords' needs.

Property Management Solution organizes and tracks tenant information, rental income and expenses, maintenance activities, and vacancy listings and generates important reports to paint a full financial picture of your rental properties. In addition, it provides the following benefits:

- ◆ Streamlines time consuming property management tasks
- ◆ Provides free web page template and hosting for use with prospective and current tenants
- ◆ Captures all key property, unit, lease, and tenant information for easy retrieval
- ◆ Increases tenant satisfaction by providing convenient web statements, requests, notices, and more

- ◆ Offers improved control over service and maintenance requests with real-time feedback to tenants
- ◆ Saves time by tracking income and expenses using IRS recognized categories reported on Tax Schedule E
- ◆ Gives tenants access to their account information online, 24 hours a day, 7 days a week

Our research at CompleteLandlord.com shows the vast majority of landlords want a simple and easy-to-use system to help them reduce the headaches and paperwork associated with the day-to-day operations of rental property. Who wouldn't agree? The problem is, before now, many existing property management systems that were on the market fell short because they were either too expensive for most landlords or too complicated to use without a property management team to offer support.

Christine Matson, a CompleteLandlord.com editor explains, "In response to numerous requests from our site's more than 70,000 members, our team of landlords has developed what we believe to be a breakthrough property management tool that we, ourselves, are excited to use."

The CompleteLandlord.com Property Management Solution is included free for all Premium Members as part of their annual membership.

Introduction to Property Management

CHAPTER 1

The Benefits of Managing Properties

Once you start buying and renting out property, it won't take long to figure out that there is definitely a "third leg" of the stool that you're sitting on: the one that handles the repair, maintenance, upkeep, and tenant relations on those properties. It's not enough to simply buy a property, fill it with warm bodies, and expect it to run itself. In fact, one of the most important elements is the actual property management that goes into being a landlord.

As a landlord, you have a few choices when it comes to property management: you can handle it all yourself, you can outsource some of it to capable companies/individuals, or you can offload the majority of the work (in exchange for a fee) to a property management firm. Which route you take is highly personal in nature and depends on how much time you have on your hands and just how good you are with a hammer and a plunger.

At CompleteLandlord.com, we have years of experience in the property management field, both firsthand and through the eyes of property management firms that are hired to handle the tasks. In this book, we will share with you the nitty-gritty details of managing properties, help you make the best possible decisions when it comes to marketing and filling your homes with tenants, walk you through some of the most important legal/business details, and help you select a property management firm that best suits your situation.

> **IMPORTANT NOTE**
> If you're starting out on the road to landlording with a single property that's located a reasonable distance from your primary home, then you'll probably want to start out with the do-it-yourself (DIY) approach. This will save you money and help you learn the ropes of property management firsthand.

Taking the Plunge

The move into property management can be a lucrative one, when done right. Instead of sinking money into the stock market, hoping that it will pay off at the right time (namely, when you need it for retirement), you can rest assured that owning and renting properties is a solid, income-generating investment strategy that many individuals overlook while plowing their cash into stocks, bonds, and 401(k)s.

 But before you dive into it, be sure to do your homework to find out what it's really like to manage properties. Despite what you may have heard, there is a lot to know and learn, and the job requires some work (or help from reliable folks who can do some or all of the work for you). The good news is that it is worth the effort, especially if you understand exactly what you're getting into before you start renting out your properties.

Here are some of the key benefits of managing properties for a living or to augment an existing income or incomes:

- ◆ *The investment pays for itself.* Once you've paid the down payment and closing costs and filled the space with a tenant, you can start using the monthly rent payment to cover your monthly mortgage obligation (provided the rent payment matches or exceeds your monthly mortgage bill).
- ◆ *The property's value will increase over time.* Real estate doesn't depreciate for any length of time, and with every year, it generally becomes worth more. The longer you hold your property, the better the chances are that you'll wind up making money on appreciation alone.

- *It may take 30 years...but eventually the property will be paid for.* At that point, all rent payments become profit for you, the owner, thus increasing the property's value and ability to earn income. With one or more properties paid off, you will be freed up to purchase one or more units or balance out your portfolio with other investments.
- *You can increase the value of your investment by improving it.* Depending on the condition and age of the homes in the direct vicinity, you may want to add landscaping, build on a new room, or take another step to up the value of your home through improvements. This strategy may allow you to fetch higher rental fees for the home and free up even more money for improvements (or further investments).
- *You'll become a proficient property manager.* We know that some of you may rely on a slew of repair personnel to handle both the small and major repairs at your properties, but we also know that some of you are good with a hammer and nails. Those who fall into either category will benefit from some of the self-help, home maintenance courses offered by organizations like Home Depot, and—after unclogging a few garbage disposals and replacing a couple of toilet kits—find themselves saving more of their money and becoming true property professionals.

There are certain tasks that you, as a property manager, will have to handle on a regular basis for each of your properties. They include (but aren't limited to):

- Keep the property in good working order so that it can be easily rented.
- Handle all repairs and maintenance on the property to maintain (or increase) its value.
- Keep your current tenants happy.
- Actively seek out renters to fill your vacancies.
- Respond to tenant needs.
- Handle any and all paperwork and administrative duties associated with rental property.
- Pay taxes on the profit generated by the properties.

And the list goes on. Like a primary residence—which requires a great deal of care and feeding on a regular basis—a rental property demands the same level of attention.

In addition to reading the book that you have in your hands right now, you'll want to spend some time reading both online and offline articles about renting out property and becoming a landlord. Here are some other great ways to learn the ropes from the people who are out in the field managing properties:

- Visit online forums such as those at CompleteLandlord.com, where members discuss the challenges and rewards of being landlords.
- Talk directly to other rental property owners to hear what they have to say about being landlords. (For example, speak with them about what it's like to rent out homes to students, people with disabilities, and other specialized markets.)
- Join a group or association whose membership is made up of property managers, landlords, and real estate investors.
- Read publications whose audience includes the property management crowd and that offer informational and how-to articles to these professionals.

IMPORTANT TIP

Find out early in the game how other property managers deal with vacancies and you'll have a jump on one of the biggest property management challenges!

Do It Yourself or Hire Someone?

You can outsource every aspect of landlording from painting and plumbing to showing rentals and screening applicants. Once you have a few properties in your portfolio, you may consider hiring a property management firm to handle a good portion of the work for you. Obviously, you will pay a price for this service, but there may be instances where the money is worth it. Here are some situations where a landlord might hire a management company to handle some or all property management tasks:

◆ The landlord is renting property in a distant city or state and cannot show the property or respond to tenant complaints.
◆ The landlord owns multiple properties and cannot manage them all himself or herself.
◆ The landlord is making so much money on rentals that he or she can afford a management company and still make a profit, thus leaving more time to invest in promising properties.

If you do not fall into one of these categories, consider carefully whether you want to spend the money on a management company. However, if some of the duties of landlording are just too hard for you to handle, you might consider finding a company that will take on just those tasks for you. Typical property management duties include:

◆ Advertising your property when new tenants are needed
◆ Showing the property
◆ Screening the applicants
◆ Providing all paperwork, including application and lease
◆ Collecting the rent
◆ Dealing with late payments, partial payments, and no payments
◆ Handling all bookkeeping and record keeping
◆ Maintaining the property
◆ Handling emergency repairs
◆ Enforcing policies and house rules
◆ Any other service you need

We know, it sounds great, right? Well, it may not sound so inviting once you hear how much you'll have to shell out for the manager's services. Property management firms make most of their money from maintenance, which they mark up by as much as 100 percent. By law, property managers must disclose to their clients how they make money, including any markups. Ask to see this documentation if it is not in the contract.

Are You Ready to Manage Property?

Here are a few key questions to ask yourself:

- Do I have experience managing rental property?
- Do I have a reliable way to determine fair market rent and returns on my investment property?
- Do I know and have the proper notices and legal process to deal with nonpaying tenants?
- Do I have a current lease and related agreements/forms to minimize my liability exposure, should a tenant decide to sue?
- Am I up to speed on fair housing and landlord/tenant laws in the jurisdiction(s) where my property is situated?
- Do I have relationships with service professionals and contractors who can provide around-the-clock service at reasonable prices?

Did you answer "no" to any of the above questions? If so, it might pay to hire a professional property management firm.

IMPORTANT TIP

It pays to keep your property shipshape, especially if you're using a property management firm. The worse shape your building is in, the more money a property firm will make from you.

The prices and fee structures used by property management firms vary greatly from company to company, but if you were to hire a management company to handle the complete job (all of the tasks listed on the previous page), you can expect to pay the firm 7 to 10 percent of your total rental income, with additional fees for the time-consuming task of showing property.

Understand that the percentages and prices charged by the property management firm will vary depending on the market in the area in which you rent. The bigger your property or the more properties you have, the lower your rate is likely to be. And keep in mind: everything is negotiable in real estate. You can try to talk a company into lowering its price, but be careful—if you are a good negotiator and get the company to come down 1 or 2 percent, they might spend more time trying to fill another client's vacancy and less time on your vacancies.

You Can Do It Yourself

For you DIY landlords out there, we have good news: it's entirely possible to manage rental property on your own and save the management fees that you'd have to pay out to a company. This task will of course be easiest for those of you who:

◆ Own just one or two properties
◆ Reside and/or work in close proximity to the properties
◆ Are able to handle odd jobs themselves on the weekends or in the evenings
◆ Have a Rolodex stocked with a few reliable, local service professionals (plumbers, HVAC pros, and so forth)
◆ Don't mind fielding calls from tenants
◆ Don't mind collecting rents and handling tenant relations (evictions, screenings, and so forth)

IMPORTANT TIP

Property management isn't an "all or nothing" proposition. You can handle some of it on your own and find one or more outside firms to take on those tasks that you either can't or won't be able to cover on your own.

Before You Go

Let it be said that owning and managing rental property isn't easy, but it certainly is profitable and enjoyable on many fronts for those who take the time to plan and execute effective strategies *before* diving in. In this book, we'll show you how to leverage your current expertise to create a property management plan that will help you be as profitable and successful as possible.

We'll start by showing you what it takes to be a property manager and let you make your own choice about whether to handle it on your own or outsource some or all of the tasks to an outside entity.

2

The Skills, Aptitude, and Attitudes of Successful Property Managers

Just like everyone is not cut out to be a teacher, lawyer, or doctor, not everyone has what it takes to be a property manager. There are tenants to screen, references to check, properties to maintain, checks to collect, property tax and mortgage loan payments to mail, and many other tasks to cover on a regular basis for each property. It takes a certain person to handle all of these tasks. In this chapter, we'll look at the skills, aptitude, and attitude that are necessary in order to be a successful property manager.

From the Beginning

First let's take a detailed look at what it takes to run a rental property. You will need certain resources, qualities, contacts, and preparations to succeed at making money on your property without running yourself ragged. One basic rule to keep in mind is that every task or aspect of landlording will either cost you time, effort, or money out of your pocket.

IMPORTANT TIP

You can take the time to do your own accounting or you can hire a professional bookkeeper to do it for you. If you do not have the skills for a task, or if you cannot afford the time, consider hiring outside help.

That's right. Being a property manager requires time commitment. At a minimum, you need to run your rental business, even if that means just giving other people orders to carry out the work. But it is likely that as a new owner, you will be doing all the work yourself. If you hold a full-time job, make sure you are ready to devote some of your off hours to your property management duties. If you own just a few rental properties, you should be able to do what needs to be done in the evenings and on weekends. If you are working with a spouse or partner, this will be even easier. And if your full-time job offers flexible hours, that too will help.

Take the Quiz

A good starting point for property managers is the same place that new business owners across all industries should use to launch their ideas: taking an entrepreneurial quiz. Here are 11 key questions to ask yourself right now:

1. Like most successful entrepreneurs, am I an optimist and a risk taker?
2. Do I have the self-starter determination to get this business going and the discipline to keep it on track?
3. Do I work hard?
4. Can I take responsibility for my own actions?
5. Am I a good problem solver?
6. Am I organized?
7. Do I have the physical stamina to work long hours?
8. Am I willing to work weekends and evenings, if necessary?
9. Can I finance this business myself if my properties are vacant for any period of time?
10. Will my family be supportive of my entrepreneurial efforts?
11. Do I have the basic skills required to start and successfully run a business, or do I have access to a mentor who can help me through the critical early stages?

If you answered yes to more than half of the questions, consider yourself a good candidate for property manager of the year. If you answered no to five or more questions, don't despair. You may simply need to change your approach to work; your mindset; and your way of managing tasks, challenges, and problems.

> It's easy to handle everything myself, especially because all my properties are in the same area. I have more flexibility with my [work] hours than most people, so I can make appointments in the middle of the day.
>
> —Mark Berlinski, owner of rental properties in Chicago, Illinois

Not counting the scouting and purchase of new rental properties, your time as a property manager will be spent on the following tasks:

◆ Advertising and showing property
◆ Screening potential tenants
◆ Moving in tenants (organizing rental agreement, keys, house rules, etc.)
◆ Collecting/depositing rents, paying bills, and other accounting tasks
◆ General maintenance and cleaning of the exterior of property
◆ Maintenance and repairs on each unit
◆ Tenant communications, as necessary
◆ Renewing leases or starting over with advertising property
◆ Staying informed on landlording laws, policies, rents, and advice

Just how much time each of these tasks will take depends on the state of your property and how efficient you are. But you can see from this list that most of these tasks can be handled on weekends or in the evenings. And you can shave time off most of these duties with the advice in this book. For starters, here are a few tips on how to reduce the number of hours you spend on your regular property management duties:

◆ Have tenants mail rent or set up a direct debit to your tenants' checking accounts or credit cards. Do not waste time collecting checks in person.
◆ Schedule a time once a month when you sit down and pay all your bills and settle your accounts. Make this date about a week after rents are due so you can see immediately if a check is late.
◆ Batch as many property management–related phone calls as you can and make them in one sitting.

- Set up a weekly and/or monthly maintenance schedule so you can batch small repair jobs to avoid multiple trips—your time is money!
- Bring something to do while you are waiting to show a unit or meet a repairman. If the person you are meeting is late or does not show, you will not have wasted time. Make phone calls, do paperwork, or check out the unit or building for necessary repairs and/or improvements.

Successful property managers treat their rental business like a business, not a hobby. One of the most basic steps you can take in this direction is to set up separate accounts for your new business. Open a new checking account and deposit rent checks in this account and use it to pay any related costs. This is an easy way to keep track of your rental income and expenses. It also keeps your personal money out of the mix, as it should be.

IMPORTANT TIP

Consider setting up a separate savings account or money market account to hold security deposits. This money, which tenants turn over as part of their rental agreement, is to be held by the landlord to cover expenses such as skipped rent or damages.

Many states require property managers to keep security deposits in a separate account and, if some or all of the deposit is returned to the tenant, to provide the interest as well. Check your state law on this or check with your local landlord association or housing authority.

What Does It Take?

A successful property manager—in particular one who is the do-it-all-yourself type—needs to have certain skills and personality traits. Here's a look at some of the key attributes of successful property managers.

◆ *Organized and detail oriented:* A property manager needs to keep track of dozens of details, including accounting, record keeping, scheduled maintenance, and so on. If you are not good at staying on top of details, find a system that shapes your schedule and your to-do list.

◆ *Good with numbers:* You will need to track several bank accounts and make sound decisions on spending and making money, including calculating how much rent you can charge and how to make a profit.

◆ *Good people skills and intuition:* Can you tell when someone is trying to manipulate you? Are you skilled at settling arguments and deflecting anger? Property managers need to know how to read and handle current and prospective tenants.

◆ *Handy around the house:* Most maintenance issues are small—stopping a toilet from running all night or tightening doorknobs. Handling these quick fixes yourself will save you a lot of money. If you do not know how to handle basic maintenance, learn! Take a class, read some books, or ask a handy friend for help.

◆ *Patient…yet firm:* As a property manager, you're likely to hear some whining and complaining on the part of your tenants. It just comes with the territory. The best professionals are the ones who can listen patiently, and then come up with solutions that wind up being win-win for both parties. In other words, you don't want to be overly accommodating, but at the same time you don't want to isolate your tenants. It's a fine line, and one that you'll learn to walk successfully as you pave your way in the industry.

In This Corner

According to the Institute of Real Estate Management (IREM), the licensing body for Certified Property Managers (CPMs), the most valuable attributes of a property manager include the following. Yes, we know it's a sales pitch for using CPMs, but the information can serve as a benchmark for you as you shape your own career as a property manager:

◆ *Knowledge of the real estate industry:* When a CPM manages your property, you get someone who is up to date on the latest

In This Corner (*Continued*)

trends in real estate. As a professional, CPM members must complete numerous hours of education to earn their designation. But learning doesn't stop there. All CPM members must meet a continuing education requirement to retain their designation and have access to the latest industry information through educational courses, publications, and the IREM web site.

- *Management expertise:* Experience is one of the defining qualities of a CPM. Candidates for the designation must have a minimum of five years of effective full-time decision-making activity in real estate management before earning the designation. The average CPM member has more than 18 years of real estate management experience. CPM members manage over $879 billion in real estate assets. They manage approximately 10.2 million residential units and 8 billion net square feet of commercial space. They are entrusted with some of the most visible and valuable real estate in the world.

- *Financial acumen:* Having a CPM member managing your property means that you have someone who is versed in more than just fixing the plumbing and collecting the rent. The training and testing a property manager must complete to earn the designation means that your investment will be run as an investment. CPMs are equally as comfortable justifying rent increases to your tenants as they are calculating and maximizing your return on investment.

For the Non-Do-It-Yourself Types

So, you're not going to handle property management on your own? No problem. In Chapter 8, you'll find detailed information on how to select a firm to help you with your landlording business. Put simply, you'll want to look for a company with credentials, references, and a track record—preferably in the types of units that you're renting out. In other words, if a firm specializes in condos, then you probably would want to think twice about using it to manage your three single-family home rentals.

IMPORTANT TIP

Membership in the local apartment/trade associations can be a good indicator of a reputable property management firm, but it doesn't always guarantee a good choice. Check with your state's Department of Real Estate or other licensing body to make sure the firm has a clean record before making your selection.

As you have read, there are certain skills and aptitudes that every property manager should have if he or she wants to succeed in the rental business. By incorporating your own strengths into the mix and augmenting them with the information you'll learn in this book, the valuable insights available on CompleteLandlord.com, and other educational resources, you'll be able to develop a plan for success.

CHAPTER 3

Build a Winning Strategy, Plan, and Team

We're not going to argue the point that some property managers prefer to learn the ropes as they go along, never taking the time to build strategies, plan ahead, or assemble support teams. Maybe they inherited the property in question and were thrown headlong into the new career, or maybe they "fell" into a windfall and needed somewhere solid to invest it. Whatever the motive, these types of owners are the exception rather than the rule.

For the rest of us, there are some tried-and-tested strategies that we can rely on to achieve success as property managers, and the first one is coming up with a long-term plan for reaching your goals. One of the best ways to get a jump on your property management venture is by writing down (or keying into a computer) a business plan, regardless of how brief or light it may be right now.

You can use some of the points taught in business planning 101 to start thinking about your plan, such as:

- ◆ What service or product does your business provide and what need does it fill?
- ◆ Who are the potential customers for your product or service and why will they purchase it from you?
- ◆ How will you reach your potential customers?
- ◆ Where will you get the financial resources to start your business?

As fundamental as they may seem, these four core components are critical to your business success as a property manager. The key is to know your product or service, your customers, how to reach them, and what resources you'll need to get there. As a property manager: Your product is the property and the support you provide as the owner. Your customers are your tenants. You will reach them through any number of marketing techniques. And you will fund your company either out of your own pocket, through a mortgage, or through other financing means.

Taking Stock

Here's a handy worksheet that you can use to answer some key questions about yourself and your property management business:

1. Why did I get into property management? (Were the motives financial in nature, were you looking for a new career, are you building a nest egg for retirement?)

   _____

   _____

   _____

2. What steps have I taken so far to achieve the goal(s) outlined in question 1?

   _____

   _____

   _____

3. Have I created a mission statement for my business? If not, start crafting one here by answering the questions: Who am I, what am I trying to accomplish, and what do I value?

   _____

   _____

   _____

4. How do I measure success in the industry, and what specific steps do I need to take to reach that level of success as a property manager?

   _____

   _____

   _____

5. How successful have I been so far in the business, and am I taking the steps outlined above to achieve my goals? Or, have I skipped steps along the way, thus lessening my chances to reach my success goals?

_____

_____

_____

6. What type of marketing plan do I have in place, and does it include marketing efforts that are cohesive and productive?

_____

_____

_____

7. Where do I stand financially right now? What level of cash reserves do I have to cover my business and personal expenses for the next four to six months?

_____

_____

_____

8. In what ways do other people in my life (such as a spouse and/or children) rely on me financially?

_____

_____

_____

Once you've made mental notes or jotted down answers to each of these questions, you'll also want to take some time to assess your answers and use them to help figure out:

◆ Where you stand right now
◆ Where you want to be professionally in the next 6 to 12 months
◆ Where you want to be, both professionally and personally, in 5 to 10 years

Your answers to the first two questions will give you a solid foundation to work with, even if you haven't yet laid that groundwork. Take the time to figure out the "whys" of your career choice. It could have been as simple as a friend telling you how great you would be at it, and that's fine. Then, look at the steps you've taken so far—no matter how small—to turn that idea into a reality.

The Next Step

Once you've taken stock of your business and personal situation, you'll be able to start planning your success in an industry where the rewards that come from hard work and smart investments can be plentiful. To get the most out of your planning, you'll want to follow these basic guidelines:

◆ *Start at square one.* Begin with some business planning basics and outline your overall plan first before going back and beefing up areas of most concern for your particular situation.

◆ *Do your homework.* Put some time into researching your market, your potential customers, and your own financial situation to come up with a realistic picture of where you are right now, where you want to be, and how you're going to get there.

◆ *Write it down.* Don't try to commit this one to memory. Jot down notes as you think through your situation and your future goals and dreams, then use those notes to create a written business plan.

◆ *Network, but do your own thing.* You can learn a lot from existing property managers, but no single professional's plan is going to be right for another. As you pick the brains of those around you for ideas, cull those that sound like they would be most applicable to you and discard the rest. Then, use the best of the best to develop your own plan.

◆ *Update regularly.* Like life, a business plan is a work in progress. You'll want to review your overall plan at least yearly, if not on a quarterly basis, to make sure you're on track. If you've met your goals, revise them. If you're much further off than you thought you would be, you may want to make the goals more attainable and tangible.

◆ *Make the time for it.* The best part about business planning is that it costs little more than time. And while it's true that new property managers are usually time strapped, trying to start their careers, find customers, and make money, it will pay to go through this early planning exercise before you get too far into it.

 By spending the time now to formulate a plan for success, you'll be much better armed when the point comes to make important decisions that result in achieving success, attaining your goals, and ultimately, reaping the financial rewards of being a property manager.

Building Blocks

Here are three key elements not to overlook in your property management business plan:

1. *Budget:* Start with a basic personal budget so you know what you need to survive during your first year or two in business. Then, plan a separate business budget that ties in with your own finances because the two will probably be intertwined during your start-up phase. Most importantly, be honest and realistic and gain a clear understanding of your own monthly financial needs for your first year.
2. *Goal setting:* This is a key step for new property managers who must know their goals if they expect to meet them. Outline both short-term and long-term goals that are within your grasp. This will inspire you to work harder and more efficiently.
3. *A support team:* Your support team is vital to your success and will help you in more ways than you can imagine as your property management venture progresses. (See the next section of this chapter for more details on creating your own support team.)

Building a Team

As the owner of one or more properties that are rented out to tenants, you simply cannot operate on your own and expect your business to grow and thrive. Those who opt to do it all themselves often wind up being labeled slumlord or other derogatory names. They spread themselves too thin and are unable to keep up with even the most basic day-to-day operational elements of being a landlord.

Successful real estate investing is all about teamwork, which means you'll need to start looking around for team members to help you round out your real estate strategy. In this chapter, the experts at CompleteLandlord.com will show you why this is so important and how to go about finding the best possible people to work with.

For starters, here are just a few things you'll need to understand (or find someone who does and add him or her to your team) simply to invest successfully in real estate:

- ◆ Contracts
- ◆ Paperwork

- ◆ Financing for the single purchase
- ◆ Financing involved with being part of a larger group doing something together, such as land acquisition, infrastructure loans, or construction loans
- ◆ Filing a changed-use form when necessary
- ◆ Obtaining entitlements
- ◆ Getting building permits
- ◆ The construction process
- ◆ Property management

As you can see, going it alone in real estate investment isn't only foolish, but it's also completely unnecessary. There are myriad professionals out there who are willing to lend their time and expertise to your cause, and it's up to you to take advantage of these valuable resources. At a minimum, your investment team should include:

- ◆ A real estate agent
- ◆ A mortgage broker or lender
- ◆ A real estate lawyer
- ◆ A Certified Public Accountant
- ◆ A certified inspector
- ◆ A real estate appraiser
- ◆ A property and casualty insurance agent

Once you've become a landlord, your team will also comprise:

- ◆ A property manager (if you aren't handling it yourself)
- ◆ A stable of reliable contractors and service providers
- ◆ A restoration service (for storm and vandalism remediation)
- ◆ Pest control
- ◆ A locksmith
- ◆ A window replacement/repair contractor
- ◆ An HVAC contractor
- ◆ A roofer

These individuals and/or companies will help make your property management experience more rewarding and successful, despite the fact that each will command a fee for services. Let's say you want to invest in real estate, but you have a full-time career. You're good at what you do. You enjoy your work, and it provides you with a steady paycheck. But this work is separate from your business as a real estate investor and landlord. The combination of skills necessary to get a team together to do the kind of analysis necessary for wise real estate investing isn't sensible for one person. So get your team together, and begin reaping the rewards.

Rounding Out the Team

The individuals you select for your team will depend on the depth of your own knowledge and skills. If you come up short in any area, you'll want to acquire the missing parts from service providers in the marketplace. If you know a lot about real estate investment, but aren't handy, then a Rolodex filled with the names of good plumbers and handymen will be more valuable than one chock full of real estate professionals.

To achieve success as quickly as possible, we want you to start filling the gaps in your team as early as possible. Being proactive will put you in a much better position and prevent you from having to run around putting out fires on the fly as they come up. Instead of going into the process blindly, don't be afraid to shell out a few bucks for some good professional help that will be valuable right now—particularly for the first few properties that you will manage. These professionals will assist you on your long-term path to success.

SECTION TWO

Operations

CHAPTER 4

Beyond Record Keeping: The Importance of Systems

As you've already learned from earlier chapters of this book, you can run your property management business by the seat of your pants by adopting the reactive, I'll-handle-the-fires-as-they-come-up mentality that many entrepreneurs adopt. Or, you can take a more systematic approach by putting systems in place that will facilitate your success as a property manager.

Lucky for you, you have technology working on your side. In years past, property managers had to cobble systems together to handle everything from tenant screening to rent collection to evictions. Some of the systems were manual, some were automated, and some were a mix of the two. None were as efficient as the tech-based options that are at your fingertips as a modern-day property manager.

Here at CompleteLandlord.com for example, we recently launched a new, online property management system available to all of our site's premium members. The program helps eliminate the excessive burden of paperwork associated with managing rental properties and is easy to use, simple to navigate, and appropriate for rental property owners with one to one thousand units due to its unique, scalable design.

Because it's an online platform, our system allows property managers to access their rental property information from any Internet location, thereby providing the optimum flexibility all landlords need. It organizes and tracks tenant information, rental income and expenses, maintenance activities, and vacancy listings and generates important reports to paint a full financial picture of your rental properties.

We came up with this solution in answer to a common request from property managers: the need for a simple system that can reduce the headaches and paperwork associated with day-to-day operations of rental property. Up until now, many existing property management systems on the market fell short because they were either too expensive for most landlords or too complicated to use without a property management team to support them.

Why You Need a System

Keeping accurate records for a rental property is essential for any property manager. One of the most basic reasons you should keep accurate records involves your personal and/or business taxes and the fact that you'll have to refer back to your records when filing your taxes. You'll also want to maintain accurate records to ward off any discrimination claims, misunderstandings regarding a property's condition, and myriad other reasons that may come up.

IMPORTANT TIP

Maintain a log of all payments that you receive from each of your tenants. Also, consider giving out either a payment booklet or a hard copy of a rental bill to each tenant, to make yours (and their) record keeping that much easier.

Be sure to retain receipts and documentation for your rental property expenses during the year. These expenses include, but aren't limited to:

◆ Maintenance work
◆ Investments in equipment
◆ Repairs

♦ Purchases (such as furniture or new fixtures)
♦ Cleaning costs
♦ Transportation costs (for you)

When it comes to your individual tenants, you'll want to maintain a separate file for each of them, and you'll want to retain those files for five years after a tenant moves out. The minimum amount of paperwork in each of those files should include:

♦ A copy of the rental application
♦ A current reference list (to be used to track down tenants who might abandon their responsibilities)
♦ A copy of the signed lease agreement
♦ An initialed copy of the walk-through checklist
♦ An ongoing record of rental payments
♦ Any and all correspondence sent to or received from the tenant
♦ Current business, cellular, and home telephone numbers
♦ Documentation on any trust account established and any interest paid on security deposits

The more tenants you have, the more complete and accurate your files will need to be to run your property management firm successfully. It's easy enough to remember the Smiths' home phone number when they are the only tenants you have, but as you continue to invest and achieve success in the field, it will be much more difficult to remember the numbers of the 12 tenants who are living in your multiunit apartment building.

Storage Options

Exactly how you document and store this paperwork is up to you. If you're the type of person who stores receipts in a shoebox, then a $49 filing cabinet and box of file folders (one for each tenant) will do. The tech-savvy may opt for a more sophisticated system of scanning the documents and storing them electronically for quick access at a later date. It's purely a personal choice and one that will depend on your level of comfort with technology and the number of properties/tenants that you're managing.

By establishing solid systems now, when your portfolio is new, you'll be adopting good record-keeping habits for your growing business.

Don't Overlook These

In addition to the basic record-keeping requirements listed in the last section of this chapter, you'll also want to keep:

- *Damage logs:* Photograph your empty rental unit *before* your next tenant moves in, and make notes of any damage you discover. You can use the dated logs, videotapes, and still photos to prove at a later date that a tenant has damaged your property.
- *Information on specific properties:* For each of your rental units, maintain a file that includes the deed, mortgage information, and a copy of your insurance policy.

IMPORTANT TIP

You may want to keep the information on your specific properties (deed, mortgage, and insurance) under lock and key in a fireproof safe, just in case.

Sample System

As you learned earlier in this chapter, there are software programs available on the market that can help property managers handle their businesses. Some programs will take care of everything from checking tenant references to handling monthly rental record keeping.

IMPORTANT TIP

As a property manager, you may be able to deduct the cost of property management software as a business expense.

One software option, for example, allows you to see who has and hasn't paid rent this month, including partial payments and late fees. It also stores tenant contact information, lease terms, security deposits, and payment histories; organizes deductions by Schedule E categories and flags expenses you're unsure about; and allows you to view and compare property performance to get the most from your investments.

The time spent inputting data into such a system may seem overwhelming, but the ability to compare property performance with just the push of a button, or find out exactly who owes you what with just the click of a mouse, can make your job as property manager that much easier.

Start Now

Regardless of which system you choose—manual, automated, or a little of both—the idea is to get comfortable using it on a regular basis...and not just when you have to. By filing documents when they're signed, inputting check numbers and amounts into your software system when you receive them, and printing reports on a regular basis, you'll be laying the groundwork for a successful (and much less stressful) property management business.

5

Property Maintenance, Repairs, and Construction

As a property manager, one of your biggest jobs is going to be maintaining and repairing your rental units. This means you can either buckle on that tool belt and hit the street on weekends, ready to tackle projects of all sizes at your properties, or you can outsource the tasks to a competent professional for a fee. Alternatively, you can handle the smaller jobs on your own and offload the larger tasks to those professionals. It's your choice, and it depends largely on your level of handiness, the condition of your properties, your experience at handling such projects, and how much time you have in your schedule to devote to such tasks.

In this chapter, we'll walk you through some of the basic areas that you'll need to pay attention to as a conscientious property manager and help you prioritize your time and budget in a way that assists you in continuing to generate income while not running yourself into the ground during your first few years as a landlord.

General Maintenance

Nearly every municipality has housing codes that landlords must follow, and most of them center around maintaining your property in a way that ensures that occupants won't be subject to housing conditions that are dangerous; hazardous; or detrimental to life, health, or safety. For most property managers, the requirements are common sense. For others, there are municipal laws and recourse to keep them on track.

Housing code violations are typically dealt with directly by a municipality representative. If a tenant complains to the municipality that you have failed to comply with the local housing code, building inspectors will visit your property. The inspectors may take action if the property is not being lawfully maintained, such as requiring you to make necessary repairs, pay a fine, or both. In extreme cases, such as lack of running water or heat in the winter, the property could be condemned and the tenants told to leave.

IMPORTANT TIP

To avoid potential housing code violations, make sure you've reviewed your local housing codes *before* filling your properties with tenants. Pick up a copy from your local or state housing offices to keep on file, or visit the Internet to see if codes are posted online.

Under most housing codes, residential rental properties must have:

◆ A heating system that is in working order and provides an adequate supply of heat to the property
◆ Lighting sufficient to allow typical indoor activities
◆ Adequate ventilation
◆ Suitable facilities for food preparation and cooking
◆ Sinks with hot and cold running (and sanitary) water
◆ A flush toilet
◆ Facilities for bathing
◆ A private entrance
◆ A means of escape in case of fire
◆ A working smoke alarm (in some cities and states, more than one)

Remember that these are the minimum requirements that your properties must meet in order to rent them out without violating fair housing codes. Your properties will either go beyond these necessities to include various other amenities or they won't be desirable places to live for prospective tenants.

Who Handles What?

As property manager, you're required to provide rental units that meet basic structural, health, and safety standards (as outlined in the previous section). If these are not met, a tenant may have defense for not paying the rent. Once a renter moves into your building, you and the tenant share joint responsibility for the maintenance and repair of the unit. However, a far greater duty to maintain the premises lies with you as the landlord.

That's because as a landlord, you provide a "warranty of habitability" that applies to all residential rentals, whether under a lease or a rental agreement (periodic tenancy). When people talk about an express warranty of habitability, it simply means that the rental agreement states the landlord is responsible for maintaining the premises and making repairs. The landlord must also ensure there are no latent defects in the premises that are hazardous to the life or safety of the tenant when the tenancy starts.

To prevent future problems, examine your property thoroughly before each lease begins. It is also a smart move to photograph all areas of the property, paying close attention to the condition of the flooring and appliances. These items are easily damaged and are costly to repair or replace. If you find damage to the property beyond normal wear and tear, your tenant should be charged for the repair costs. Photographs can serve as proof of damage if there is a discrepancy.

In addition to basic maintenance responsibilities, most state laws require tenants to inform you immediately of any defects that may be your responsibility. Make periodic visits to keep tabs on your tenants' general maintenance of their unit.

Preventing Problems

"An ounce of prevention." We all know the adage, but experience is sometimes the best teacher. Seasoned landlords know it is far less expensive to maintain what they have than to repair or replace it. Preventive maintenance is the key to ensure problems are addressed before they become emergencies.

A good time to begin an ongoing maintenance program is *before* new tenants move into a unit. During this inspection, be sure to check all:

- ◆ Faucets
- ◆ Showerheads
- ◆ Smoke detectors
- ◆ Electrical outlets
- ◆ Light fixtures

Develop a checklist of items in advance to use as a guide during your inspection check to make sure each is in good working order.

IMPORTANT TIP

One way to avoid unnecessary repairs is to educate new tenants on the mechanical workings of the rental unit. Show them how to test the smoke detector and the proper way to use the garbage disposal to avoid jams and breakdowns. This is also a good time to jointly note any preexisting issues, such as stains on the carpet or scratches on the kitchen counter.

Landlord Insights

Clean the coils in the back of your refrigerator with a brush regularly to reduce electricity usage and extend the life of your refrigerator.

—Jack Butler, independent landlord

Open Lines of Communication

It could be lack of concern or the fear of being labeled a complainer, but many tenants will not bother you with minor maintenance issues. For example, a small drip in the bathroom ceiling may seem a small annoyance to a tenant but could indicate a much larger problem that should not be left unattended. Explain to tenants that no problem is too small to bring to your attention and that you want to address even minor issues before they become bigger.

 One way to keep tabs on routine maintenance issues is to conduct regularly scheduled safety inspections during the year. One or two per year will probably suffice, but it is a good idea to inform all tenants at lease signing of this policy.

For ongoing repairs, let your tenants know they need to contact you immediately when they notice a problem so that you can address it. Remind them of your contact numbers, and be responsive when they do call. Many landlords end up with big repair issues that could have easily been avoided if only the tenant would have called the landlord when it was just a small repair.

Rolling Out the Red Carpet

Carpeting can be a substantial investment for most property owners. Unfortunately, many times tenants with pets do not properly maintain and care for the carpets in their units. Carpet pet odor can be so strong that there is no alternative but to replace the entire carpet and pad. This is especially true for cat urine, which is highly concentrated and difficult to remove completely from carpeting.

But before you throw out the carpet, examine its condition thoroughly and consider replacing just the pad underneath and shampooing the carpet. (Leave the shampooing to professionals; however, because most now have effective enzyme-based treatments to remove even the toughest odors.)

Replacing the pad is nearly always required when dealing with pet urine because the pad will retain moisture and odors even after the carpeting is dry. If you shampoo the carpet without replacing the pad, the smell will eventually resurface, and you will have to address the issue again.

Another key step to take is to apply a sealant, such as Kilz, to the base flooring before you install the new pad. Strong odors will often soak into the base flooring, including concrete. If you skip this step, the smell could come back.

Landlord Insights

As a landlord with only three properties, I have decided to extend to the existing three-year tenants a carpet cleaning invitation to coincide with their lease renewal. This will encourage them to clean up a bit, feel better about the place, maybe rearrange furniture, and enjoy their home all over again. This helps maintain my property too.

—Independent landlord

Procurement

Maintenance and repair costs can take an unwelcome bite out of any property manager's budget. Some may overspend, fearing bigger problems later; others may try to get by spending too little, leading to costlier repairs later on. It can be a difficult balancing act, but there are ways to cut costs. Consider the following strategies:

◆ Supplies are a routine expense for landlords, many of whom save costs by shopping at big-box retailers. Stock up on supplies when sales occur and keep a few extra items on hand so you are not running back and forth to the store.

◆ If you happen to live in a larger city, hardware wholesalers are another good retail option. As a business owner, you may qualify to participate in a network enabling you to buy maintenance supplies at significantly lower costs.

◆ If you are not familiar with any outlets, check the hardware (wholesale) section of your Yellow Pages or talk to contractors who have the inside scoop.

When it comes to larger expenses, such as lighting, fixtures, and appliances, standardizing your choices is a smart move to save you time and money. For example, paint all units with the same brand, color, and type of paint. This way, when you make touch-ups, you can be confident the paint will match. Likewise, use the same plumbing, lighting, and hardware fixtures wherever possible. This allows you to easily interchange parts that need replacing. Save functioning parts from failed items to use for future repairs.

> **Landlord Insights**
>
> At my properties, I install compact fluorescent bulbs in lieu of incandescent bulbs to substantially reduce electricity usage and cut down on the need for bulb change-outs.
>
> —Mark Knefelkamp, independent landlord

One of the best ways to handle the procurement aspect of your property management role is by shopping around, using tools like the

Internet to compare prices, quality, and value. Ordering from the Internet can be a good option, provided you don't need the equipment, materials, or supplies quickly. Be sure to factor in any shipping costs when shopping online, because those costs may offset any savings you may realize by not picking up the materials at your local Home Depot.

Landlord Insights

When rehabbing a property from long distance, conduct conference calls with your work crew once a week or every few days. This is a great way to manage. Check out FreeConference.com, which provides free conference lines for you and your team.

—Independent landlord

Grease Trap

According to a recent survey by CompleteLandlord.com, the most frequent complaints handled by landlords are plumbing related. To head off problems before they start, provide your tenants with the following information to prevent clogged drains:

- Avoid pouring grease down the kitchen sink—it collects along the sides of the pipe and food particles stick to it, clogging the drain. Instead of putting it down the drain, pour grease into cans and throw them in the garbage.
- Put coffee grounds in the garbage, not down the drain.
- Run cold water while grinding food in the disposal to flush food particles down the pipe.
- Pour a kettle of boiling water down the drain once a week to melt any fat or grease that has collected.
- Periodically, pour a half-cup of baking soda and half a cup of white vinegar down the drain. Cover the drain and let the mixture sit for a few minutes, then flush it down with a kettle of hot water.
- Never pour hot wax or chemicals, such as paint, down the drain.
- Never flush heavy paper products, such as paper towels, down the toilet.
- Periodically clean sink stoppers in all sinks and tubs to keep hair and other drain-cloggers out of the pipes.

Ask your tenants to follow these easy tips. You will make fewer trips to repair the plumbing, and your tenants will avoid the inconvenience of clogs.

Green Property Management

With the growing amount of attention being paid to global warming, conservation efforts are in full swing throughout many industries. Hotels, businesses, and industries are making changes that benefit not only the environment but also their own bottom lines in the process.

Rental property management is no different. Though small changes may not seem profound enough to have an effect, some simple energy saving methods can lower your monthly costs considerably.

Consider lighting, for example. It is important to keep common areas of the building well lit so that people feel safe and secure. Have you thought about installing timers on hallway lights?

Here are some excellent ways to help the *green* movement:

- ◆ During the daylight hours, light only every other light fixture. Then at dusk, have all of the lights come on. Consider installing motion detector lights in areas not commonly in use, such as laundry rooms and storage areas. In these common areas, you rarely count on tenants to turn off lights after they leave. A motion detector light can reduce wasted electricity.
- ◆ Water bills are another overlooked source of waste. A running toilet or a dripping faucet may be a minor annoyance to a tenant, but the wasted water leads to higher water bills for you, the landlord. Routinely check for yourself that all faucets and toilets are working properly.
- ◆ Ensure bathrooms are equipped with water-saving showerheads. Your tenants are not likely to notice any difference, and you will appreciate the water savings. Consider installing low-flow toilets, adjusting flush valves, or putting in dams on existing toilets to reduce water waste. You can also purchase water-conserving icemakers for your freezers.
- ◆ As your current appliances wear out, replace them with energy-efficient models. The initial costs of these types of appliances may be higher, but your energy costs will be significantly lower in the long run.

By doing your part (no matter how small it may seem) to help preserve the environment and decrease your property's "footprint" in this world, you'll get the benefits of that feel-good sentiment, you'll attract tenants who share your mindset, and you may even wind up saving money on energy and materials.

As you pave your way in the property management field, be sure to heed the advice you learned in this chapter from the experts at CompleteLandlord.com and its members, all of whom have valuable tips to share when it comes to property maintenance, repair, and construction. By keeping your properties well maintained, safe, and in good repair, you'll become known as a property manager who truly cares about his or her investments and the families who dwell in them.

Achieving Scale: Hiring, Training, Retaining, and Compensating Property Management Personnel

There comes a time in every property manager's life when the question "Do I need to hire help?" comes up. Maybe she wants to put her efforts on another project. Perhaps he feels the need to offload noncore tasks to another party. Or maybe the property manager is burning the candle at both ends—a feeling that many businesspeople can commiserate with at some point in their careers.

Whatever the motivating factor, the story usually ends with the property manager either hiring full-time or part-time help or offloading work to a management company. We'll cover the last option in detail in Chapter 7; here we'll discuss the task of hiring, training, paying, and retaining property management personnel.

IMPORTANT TIP

Not everyone gives in to the urge to hire help. There are those who circumvent it altogether and post successes without assistance. Others have taken the hiring route only to find out that the control freak or entrepreneur in them would rather handle things on their own, instead of spending precious time training someone else to do it. Find your own comfort level with this aspect of the business and stick with it to achieve maximum success.

Help Wanted

If you're spending a lot of time licking envelopes, running around handling odd jobs at your properties, and collecting rent checks, then you're probably not making the best use of your time as a property owner. This scenario will likely occur after you have several properties in your portfolio, and the remedy may lay in placing a help wanted ad in your newspaper or on an online job board like Monster or craigslist.com to find someone to assist you with the tasks.

One of the first considerations—before you even put that ad in the paper—is how you're going to pay this person, or these people. If you're barely scraping by with three rent checks on three properties per month, now is probably not the time to go into hiring mode. However, if you have surplus income every month, and if it's enough to support one or more part-time or full-time employees (and if having those employees means you will generate even *more* income as a result), then you'll want to consider this option.

To tell you everything you need to know about hiring and training good employees would require an entire book of its own, so we'll just stick to the some of the basics you need to know if this is the route you're going to take.

Twelve Ways to Keep Your Team Intact

1. *Be clear about what you expect.* Make sure people understand the specific outcomes that you want from them and that they fully understand their roles and responsibilities.
2. *Delegate tasks and functions appropriately.* Give people the authority along with the responsibility to do their jobs and make sure they have access to the resources needed to complete the tasks.
3. *Share information.* Particularly if the organization is going through a change (whether it is a merger, acquisition, restructuring or downsizing, or growth and expansion) share all the information you are at liberty to share; and for sensitive information you can't share, tell them that you are not at liberty to share regarding that information.
4. *Equip employees with the information they need to do their jobs.* Ask people what information they need to successfully complete their tasks. If they don't know or are not aware of what they need, be accessible to them for any questions and concerns.

> ### *Twelve Ways to Keep Your Team Intact (Continued)*
>
> 5. *Do not spin the truth.* Be straight with your people. Your credibility and trustworthiness are too important to waste. And if you are spinning the truth, most of the time, others will know or find out.
> 6. *Admit mistakes.* Create a safe environment so people will feel free to take responsibility for their errors. The last thing you need is to be blindsided by a mistake that could have been easily corrected.
> 7. *Give and receive feedback constructively.* Make sure your intent is to help not hurt, ridicule, or harm. Do so with understanding and compassion. When receiving feedback, take a deep breath, and listen for the intent and the meaning of what is being said.
> 8. *Maintain confidential information.* When someone entrusts you with proprietary information, treat the information and them with dignity and respect and keep the confidence.
> 9. *Don't gossip or backbite.* If you have an issue or concern about someone, speak directly to that person and deal with the matter at hand. Talking negatively about someone to another is divisive and kills trust within a team or group because it makes the whole work environment psychologically unsafe.
> 10. *Do not tell people how to do their jobs.* Most people want to do a good job and once they are clear on what needs to be accomplished, they will do their best work when they are given the freedom to do their jobs in their own way versus being micromanaged to death.
> 11. *Allow people to make decisions.* Give people the freedom and flexibility to make decisions when you can, particularly those decisions that affect their jobs and their lives.
> 12. *Communicate with your employees.* Involve people and seek their input for better decisions and effective implementation of solutions. If someone is inadvertently left off an e-mail list, for example, take responsibility and correct the mistake as expediently as possible.

Basic Training

With 110 properties positioned throughout the New York metropolitan area, Connecticut, and New Jersey, one property management firm has its hands full when it comes to keeping onsite employees up to speed on key issues that range from risk management to labor standards, and everything in between. Despite the challenges, the company says such training is vital to the smooth running of the firm.

The firm does regular training with staff members and relies on organizations like Institute of Real Estate Management (IREM) and Building Owners and Managers Association (BOMA) to supplement its training and information updates. The latter, for example, holds seminars and produces a compliance handbook on the Americans with Disabilities Act (ADA) and also offers information on energy compliance and other issues of concern to property managers and their on-site personnel.

Internally, personnel are also kept in the loop via memos and e-mail, typically used when quick updates need to be conveyed to the group. But not all management firms are so diligent, according to one national Human Resources expert. "Many times, the company will toss the new hire a set of keys and a list of properties and wish them well," he says. "While some larger firms take pains to make sure that people do the right things and get the right information as early in the process as possible, regional organizations may still lack the resources to create a formalized orientation and/or training program."

Handyman or Contractor?

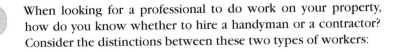 When looking for a professional to do work on your property, how do you know whether to hire a handyman or a contractor? Consider the distinctions between these two types of workers:

1. *A handyman is best for small to medium-sized jobs that require a wide range of skills and attention to detail.* These individuals are generally less expensive than contractors, but the work may take longer to complete. A handyman can do about $500 worth of work per job, per day, and often works alone or with a small crew. The benefit of this is that there is less disruption on the property. Foot traffic from a contractor's large crew on your property could be heavy.

> ### *Handyman or Contractor? (Continued)*
>
> 2. *Hire a contractor if you have a larger project, especially one that requires expertise in several areas, such as plumbing, drywall, electrical, or carpentry work.* The contractor will coordinate all professional subcontractors and the timing of their work, and you benefit from having a single contact person. Also, most major projects such as renovations and additions require building permits that are more easily secured by a contractor.

A good starting place is a policy manual that clearly states the policies and procedures that must be followed and that outlines how your firm follows those rules and what steps must be taken to ensure that the rules are indeed being adhered to. Leave room for updates (which can be sent by e-mail and inserted into the hard copy manual when warranted) and augment the manual with in-person training (such as a half-day class) when necessary.

An important aspect of the policy manual and subsequent update distribution is an individual sign-off sheet, where all employees who have read the manual sign and date that they have indeed done so. Although it sometimes creates a paperwork boondoggle in the employee's personnel folder, it eliminates any second-guessing about whether the manager/employee has been made aware of the law (if a problem or potential lawsuit arises).

IMPORTANT TIP

To create your own policy manual, visit government web sites such as the Department of Labor (www.dol.gov) or the Department of Housing and Urban Development (www.hud.gov) as the best starting point. There, you'll be sure to get the most updated and accurate information about the laws and regulations.

Peer-to-peer training, in which a knowledgeable individual trains the rest of the group on risk management and labor issues, is another good way to keep on-site personnel up to date. The best candidates to lead the training are individuals who are up to date on all of the laws and who also understand how to apply those laws in the commercial real estate setting.

From the Top Down

For on-site property management personnel training to be effective, you as the owner must not only believe in its value, but also support it 100 percent. Using labor laws as an example, you may want to create an open-door policy through which employees can approach upper-level management with questions, for example, if they are not paid adequately for time worked.

Fair Labor Standards Act Rules

Today's property managers and owners should be familiar with the recently revised Fair Labor Standards Act (FLSA), established by the U.S. Department of Labor (DOL). Prior to August 2004, it had been 50 years since the DOL had updated its "white collar" overtime regulation rules. As the primary law that affects employee payment, the FLSA's overtime pay section was amended to strengthen overtime rights for 6.7 million Americans (including 5.4 million low-wage workers) who were denied overtime under the old rules. The regulation covers the following important areas:

◆ Minimum wage
◆ Overtime pay
◆ Record-keeping requirements
◆ Child labor standards

As developed in 1938, the FLSA contained little information on or definitions of executive, administrative, or professional employees beyond the general scope of belief that they were paid more than minimum wage. At the time, the American workforce was much different than it is today in that nearly 50 percent of all employees worked in occupations directly related to manufacturing and production (blue-collar workers).

One of the FLSA's basic requirements involves determining the exemption status of each position in an organization by establishing whether an employee is exempt or nonexempt:

◆ *An exempt employee is not paid for overtime hours worked.* There are three categories under which an employee may be considered exempt. They are administrative, executive, and professional. These categories generally define an exempt employee as one who customarily and regularly exercises discretion and independent judgment in the performance of his or her duties.

Fair Labor Standards Act Rules (Continued)

♦ *A nonexempt employee is paid for all overtime hours worked.* Overtime is typically defined as any time worked over 40 hours in a workweek. Nonexempt employees generally perform functions such as routine clerical duties, maintenance work, and checking and inspecting equipment.

The FLSA revisions (also known as the FairPay rules) have put companies, managers, and trainers in a tight position as they attempt to stay on the right side of these laws, which at times can be just as confusing as the IRS tax code. Because of the new laws, for example, in order to qualify for exemptions, employees generally must meet certain tests regarding their job duties and be paid on a salary basis of not less than $455 per week. Also new is the fact that job titles alone do not determine exempt status.

One thing you'll want to keep in mind as you start filling your employee ranks is this: now you're going to become a manager. So while you're less *hands on* out in the field, you will be charged with controlling all of the details that go into hiring, training, and retaining your team members (i.e., until you can also afford to hire a human resources professional to handle that for you too!).

To achieve scale while adding new properties and tenants to your lineup, there's no doubt that you'll need help getting the job done. In the next chapter we'll look at how to outsource some or all of your property management duties to an outside firm.

Online Training Resources

Here are a few online resources for information on specific training topics:

Americans with Disabilities Act
www.ada.gov

Department of Housing and Urban Development (HUD)
    (for fair housing)
www.hud.gov/offices/fheo/index.cfm

(continued)

Online Training Resources (Continued)

National Labor Relations Board
www.nlrb.gov

The Risk Management Institute
www.irmi.com

The Wage and Hour Division of the U.S. Department of
    Labor (for minimum wage, labor standards, and FLSA)
www.dol.gov/esa/whd/

CHAPTER 7

Outsourcing Property Management

If you're tired of the hassles of being a landlord but want to keep your investments, then a property management company may be the answer. There are three different types of property management companies, each with a varying degree of involvement:

1. *Asset management companies* focus solely on the property side of being a landlord. These companies handle fact finding and decision making regarding the acquiring, holding, and selling of properties.
2. *Off-site management companies* hire and supervise on-site employees, contract any major maintenance or repairs, purchase large items, carry out evictions, and manage bookkeeping and check writing.
3. *On-site management companies* take care of the daily, site-specific tasks. They show vacant properties, select tenants, purchase smaller items, manage minor maintenance issues, collect rent, and make banking deposits.

Any combination of the three companies may be used to relieve some of the landlord burden depending on how much involvement and control you wish to retain.

First Things First

Before offloading tasks to an outside firm, analyze exactly what tasks need to be done to manage the property. Include jobs like collecting rent, cleaning empty units, rerenting them, handling repairs, snow removal, and landscaping. Next, estimate how much time is spent doing each task by each person (or by you) on a weekly basis. Multiply the time spent by each person by his or her earnings to determine how much it costs to self-manage the property.

> Successful property management agreements begin with clear expectations and good communications. Achieve both with the CompleteLandlord Property Management Form, which helps you arrange the terms of hire for a property manager to look after your property, decide what tasks will be performed by whom, and document how much the property manager will be paid. Check it out online at www .completelandlord.com/store/property-management-agreement.aspx.

Now, ask yourself the following questions:

◆ How valuable is my time (or the time of my employees who handle tenant problems and issues)?
◆ What could I be doing with the time spent managing the property?
◆ Could I be using the time that I free up to pursue another career, enjoy a hobby, or spend more time with my family?
◆ How knowledgeable am I about lease renewals, rent increases, and the current real-estate market?
◆ Am I looking to move to another area, yet still keep my current property rented out?

Even property managers who have been handling the day-to-day duties of their businesses for years are often surprised to learn that the do-it-yourself approach is costing them more (in both time and money) than an outside firm would charge. Do the math carefully to come up with a workable plan that fits well with your situation.

Can You Afford It?

Take a look at your expenses on your rental property. Besides your mortgage payments, add up your insurance, property taxes, income taxes, cost of repairs and improvements, plus any home office expenses you pay to run your landlord business.

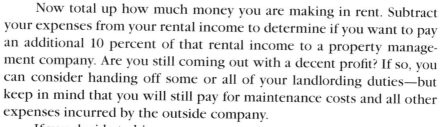

Now total up how much money you are making in rent. Subtract your expenses from your rental income to determine if you want to pay an additional 10 percent of that rental income to a property management company. Are you still coming out with a decent profit? If so, you can consider handing off some or all of your landlording duties—but keep in mind that you will still pay for maintenance costs and all other expenses incurred by the outside company.

If you decide to hire a property management company, make sure you shop around for the best value because you will find a wide range of services, quality, and price. Remember that the fees you pay to a property management company are tax deductible because they are considered a business expense.

Where to Look for a Management Company

If you are a member of a local landlord association, that group can probably recommend a property manager. Otherwise, you can ask the Institute of Real Estate Management (IREM) for some recommendations. Local chapters of the group are listed on www.irem.org.

Or you can perform a web search on your own using the terms "property management" or "rental property management" and the name of your town. You can also look in the Yellow Pages under "Real Estate Management." You can also ask your real estate agent if he or she can recommend a property manager.

When you are looking for a property management company to handle your rental property and tenants, your main priority should be finding a firm that is ethical and knowledgeable about handling property for independent landlords. Take some time to talk to representatives from each company to get a feel for their trustworthiness and their experience.

Ask These Questions

- Make a list of everything you would like the firm to do and ask if it currently handles these tasks. Ask if they will handle only part of the list, such as advertising and showing property.
- What are the costs per task? The company should have a simple fee structure. Study each cost to see if it is worth hiring out for something you can do yourself.
- Do they mark up supplies or labor for maintenance and repair work?
- Do they provide a 24/7 emergency service?
- How do they communicate with clients? Will you receive a regular report or phone call?
- Do they assign a specific person to one property? This gives you and your tenant a single point of contact.
- Can they provide references of landlords similar to you?

IMPORTANT TIP

Make sure the company is licensed. In some states, people can get a property manager's license; in others, they should have a real estate license. Also, make sure the company is bonded (insured against employee theft) and insured for liability and worker's compensation.

When you get a list of references from a property management company you are considering, make sure to call every single reference provided.

Landlord Insights

Ask each reference about his or her vacancy rates, turnaround time in renting, whether his or her reports come on time, and whether the checks come on time.

—Catherine Brouwer, founder, Blue River Properties, Memphis, Tennessee

Go Beyond Price

When you start researching property management companies, you will find that most are within 1 or 2 percent of each other in their general fees. Keep in mind that the cheapest one is not necessarily the best one—do not be attracted to a lower price or you could end up losing money. The crucial factor is finding a company that will fill your property fast with good tenants.

You'll also want to look for a company that works for a mix of different landlords. In other word, you want a property manager company that handles people like you. If you are a brand-new landlord, you want someone who manages rental property for other new landlords. If you have owned multiple properties for years, look for someone who handles landlords in similar situations. You want a company that has experience dealing with someone in your situation.

A word of caution here: you do not want a company that handles property that is too similar to yours. If you own a multiunit building, you do not want the company that is filling vacancies in an identical building down the street—all the prospective tenants are likely to end up in those apartments.

> **Landlord Insights**
>
> A landlord having his or her first experience with a property manager probably does not have a lot of units. In that case, you should look for a smaller, more personal company. You will not get any attention from a larger company.
>
> —Catherine Brouwer, founder, Blue River Properties,
> Memphis, Tennessee

Signing a Contract

If you hire a management company, it will most likely want you to sign an agreement. This document will spell out what the company will do for you and how much it will cost. Study it carefully, and if you do not think it is in your best interests, consult an attorney.

Any contract should be cancelable by either party with a 30-day written notice—for any reason. You do not want an agreement that locks you into a year or more with the company.

Most property management firms use a standardized management contract that provides that the management firm (not the owner) gets to keep the late charge and/or returned check charge. Most top-notch firms have eliminated this clause. Again, this is ironic because it is the job of the property manager to screen the tenant and enforce the rent collection in a timely manner.

Mind the Details

Property management duties vary, but most firms will prepare the unit to rent, rent the unit, collect and deposit the rent, pay any bills, prepare a monthly financial statement, and make quarterly inspections. The owner usually pays for advertising and to check the credit of prospective tenants.

Being overcharged for maintenance can be a problem. Many companies lowball the management fee and make it up on markups for maintenance. This includes high markups on labor—they may pay the maintenance person $20 per hour, but charge you $50. They may also mark up materials as much as 50 percent more than what you would pay at your local big-box store. The only way to keep from being overcharged for maintenance is to do it yourself, which doesn't work for an absentee landlord.

Weighing It Out

Landlords are a diverse bunch. Some prefer the hands-on approach and manage all the different aspects of their rental property from the process of renting, to rent collection and maintenance. To find out if you fall into this category, you should consider first whether you like to do things around the house. It usually helps if you do because this landlording approach means you could take a role in fixing some of the smaller issues that need repair in a rental home. If you don't, then you probably aren't going to be a hands-on landlord.

IMPORTANT NOTE

Occasionally good and friendly relationships with others (including tenants) can lead people to take advantage of your goodwill. Take note of how situations progress, and if you feel you're being taken advantage of, the solution would be to take a step back and treat the situation with a more business-like demeanor.

Another question you should ask is just how good are you at keeping up on maintenance? And, if a problem comes up, can you respond quickly to address it? Landlords who respond quickly are more apt to keep a good relationship with their tenants. If you're slow to respond to tenants' needs, you may develop more of an adversarial relationship with them. Once this perception is in place, it is very difficult to dispel. If you have good social skills and address issues quickly, the relationship with your tenants can be more positive.

Part of what determines just how much work you will need to contribute is the type of property you purchase. Remember the things you are good at when deciding on a purchase. If you're afraid of heights you may want to stick with ranch-style homes because there may be a time when you need to go up on the roof for repairs.

Of course, this type of landlord relationship requires a time commitment. If time is something you are in short supply of, you may want to minimize the impact by purchasing an investment property that is not too far from your current home. Then there is the time that will be required for maintenance and repair in addition to the management issues.

With the information you've learned in the last two chapters, you should have a pretty good idea of what it takes to run one or more rental properties and whether you have the time and drive to handle it yourself. If not, don't despair. There are plenty of reputable property management firms out there that are ready and willing to handle the task in exchange for a fee.

Tenants

CHAPTER 8

Marketing Vacancies/Setting Rents and Terms

So you know the basics of what it takes to be a property manager, where to find help with your new venture, and how to achieve scale in the landlording business. Now it's time to learn how to market your properties, find suitable tenants, keep them happy, and handle any problems that come up while they're residing at your rental property.

That's right! You're officially ready to start your search for the perfect tenants for your new rental property. That is, as long as your property is in move-in condition—meaning completely clean, with everything in good repair, with a tidy exterior—and if you would not be ashamed to take your own mother on a walk-through of the property.

IMPORTANT NOTE

Before you get started, make sure you're ready to show the property. Do you have time to set aside to meet prospects? Do you have the proper applications and paperwork ready to hand out? If not, take the time to get these things in order before you jump in.

If you and your property are ready to start showing immediately, then you can begin the process of seeking a tenant. Your first step is to advertise that you have property to rent. There are several ways to do this, and you should use a combination of methods rather than relying on a single one. You want to get the word out in as many ways as possible, and as cheaply and effectively as possible.

Remember, you are in this for the long haul. Keep track of how you find your best tenants and continue to use those methods. If your newspaper ads have not pulled in anyone in the past five years, maybe you can stop using them or try a different paper.

Bare Bones Information

Anyone searching for a home will need to know the following to bother contacting you for a showing or for more information:

- Location (not the exact address, but rather the street name, intersection, commuter train stop, or neighborhood)
- Number of bedrooms and bathrooms
- Price and whether utilities are included
- When it is available

After they have eliminated properties that do not fit their needs for location, size, price, and availability, renters will be interested in these secondary factors:

- Parking/garage space
- School district (if they have kids)
- Pet policy (if they have pets)
- Laundry and amenities
- Storage

Word of Mouth

One of the best ways to fill your rental properties is free, easy, and painless...and it might yield some excellent tenants! Tell family, friends, friends of friends, and certainly, any current tenants that you have an apartment or house to rent. Tell them the basics (see "Bare Bones" box) and ask if they can recommend anyone who is looking.

If no one seems interested in helping you, consider offering a finder's fee to the individual who recommends a tenant. If you are offering this reward to an existing tenant, the finder's fee might be a discount on rent or a special service like installing a ceiling fan; otherwise, the finder's fee should be cold, hard cash—enough to interest someone without becoming a major expense to you. Maybe $30 or $40.

For example: You might ask, "Do you know of anyone who is looking for an apartment? I have a newly renovated two-bedroom available at the beginning of next month. It is in a two-flat in Bucktown, and the rent is $1,400 a month, but that includes utilities. I am offering $30 to the person who can find me a tenant—after he or she moves in, of course."

Classified Ads

Most renters begin their search for a new home in one of two ways: They read the "For Rent" section in the newspaper to see what is available or they drive around the area where they want to live looking for signs.

Let's look at how to run a classified newspaper ad. Classified ads are those little all-text ads in the paper that are divided into help wanted, homes for rent and sale, items for sale, garage sales, and so on. If you are familiar with your town (and its rental market), you should know which newspapers people use most for the classifieds. If you do not, ask around. Long-time residents—especially renters—will certainly know. Of course, cost is a consideration, but if everyone in your entire town uses a particular paper to hunt for rentals, that is the paper you should advertise in. Once you have pinpointed the newspaper(s) you should put your advertisement in, follow these steps:

1. Call the newspaper office or check its web site to find out how much it costs to run a classified ad. Chances are you will need an ad for more than a week, so find out about package deals where you can buy three or four weeks or more. The cost will depend on the newspaper's circulation and other factors, but typically publications charge per word or per character for any type of classified ad. So, the longer your ad, the more it will cost.
2. Ask if the paper has an online edition, and if so, does it automatically include classified ads there. If not, find out about the additional pricing.

3. Check the paper's deadline for ads. Typically you need to submit an ad for the Sunday paper by the previous Wednesday or Thursday.

4. Start advertising as soon as possible. Remember, you must be ready to show the property as soon as that ad runs, but the sooner you can start, the better off you will be. Either you will have plenty of lead time or you will find a tenant that much sooner.

5. Write your ad. You want to keep it short, but not so short that no one will see it. Get a copy of the classified section you are advertising in and choose an ad that is three to seven lines long. Count the number of words or characters in the ads so you will have some measure of how long it should be—then check the price of that ad to make sure it is still affordable. Shorten it as necessary. You will want to include the bare bones information mentioned earlier, as well as some other selling points, like the things that might stand out about your rental property, such as: the convenient location, its large size, or a heart-shaped Jacuzzi. Mention one or two top features in your ad to draw tenants to the next step: calling you.

6. If your ad runs for more than two weeks, consider rewriting it weekly as a way to get more attention. For example—total words, 24; total characters, 153:

Convenient but quiet Bucktown location! 2 bdrm/1 bath on side street but close to transportation, shopping, school. $1400/mo, utilities included. Avail. 9/1. Call 312.555.5555.

Signs on Property

Whether your rental property is on a quiet country lane or a bustling city block, a sign in the yard or on the door is a terrific way to advertise for a new tenant. Why? Well, many people shop for a home by location, whether they want to stay in the same neighborhood or have targeted a specific area as *the* place to be. They will notice your sign as they walk the sidewalks or drive by and take note of your property. This is effective in hot neighborhoods where schools are good or the hip people live, and equally good in out-of-the-way neighborhoods and streets.

Landlord Insights

If you have a nice apartment in a nonestablished neighborhood, signs work really well. People who do not know the neighborhood may make an appointment to see your apartment, but they do not show up because they do not like the neighborhood or it is too far from transportation. But people who already work or live in the neighborhood will not do that.
—Mark Berlinski, owner of multiple rental properties in Chicago, Illinois

Make sure your sign is neat, easy to see from the street (at least the For Rent headline), and aligned neatly, whether taped to the door of a multiunit building or posted on the yard in front of a house.

What Should Your Sign Say?

Your sign should include the same information from your classified ad, but you do not have to count characters because signs are free. Also, you can skip any description of the exterior of the property since anyone reading your sign can see it themselves. You might also include a line requesting interested parties to call, *not* knock on the door and bother the current tenants.

Example: Sign Taped to Door

FOR RENT—available Sept. 1

Spacious 2-bedroom apartment with 1 bath, living room, dining room, eat-in kitchen. Hardwood floors throughout.

Street parking available. Close to #33 bus line and interstate on-ramp; walk to shopping and Elmwood High School.

$1,400/mo, utilities included. Pets okay.

Landlord off premises—call 312.555.5555.

(It is a good idea to have tags cut into the bottom of your sign or take-away flyers with your phone number.)

Example: Sign on Lawn

FOR RENT—available Sept. 1

2-bedroom apartment with 1 bath

$1,400/mo, utilities included

Pets okay

Landlord off premises—call 312.555.5555

There is less information on the lawn sign because you want it to be readable at a glance, as people are walking or driving by.

Flyers and Handouts

Similar to posting a sign on your rental property, but a bit more proactive, is handing out flyers in the same neighborhood to increase your chances of catching people's attention. Print out or photocopy a notice on 8 ½″ × 11″ paper. Use colored paper to draw attention and consider printing two half-sheet flyers on a page and then cutting them down to make 8 ½″ × 5 ½″ flyers. You can also include a photo if you have a good one.

Whatever the design of your flyer, you will need to distribute them in either the neighborhood where your property is and/or the neighborhood where you feel your ideal tenants might be residing.

You can:

◆ Stick one under every car's windshield wiper.
◆ Slide one under every screen door.
◆ Ask local businesses if you can tape one up in their windows.
◆ Stand on a street corner and hand them out.
◆ Give a handful to family members and/or friends and ask them to distribute them.

No matter how you spread the word, you will draw attention to your property. Neighbors who do not see your sign will still get the message—and may become your next tenants.

Notices on Bulletin Boards

Another way that renters look for their next dream home is checking the bulletin boards at their local grocery store or coffee shop. Post a card with details of your rental on any bulletin board in your neighborhood and beyond. Maybe your workplace has a board. Put up a notice there (if you do not mind renting to a coworker), or check your church, your kids' school, and any community buildings for boards as well.

If you have neat handwriting, write up the description. (Some grocery stores want everyone to use the card provided so you will have to write it out.) Otherwise, post a copy of your flyer or print up descriptive index card-sized sheets on your computer. Again, colored text and/or paper will help draw attention, and providing tagged cutouts with your phone number may increase your response. Use a large For Rent headline since your card will be posted with all sorts of notices, from used motorboats for sale to free kittens. You want prospective tenants to easily see your card on the board and recognize what you are selling.

Example

FOR RENT:

2 BDRM BUCKTOWN APARTMENT

Spacious 2 bedroom, 1 bath apartment with living room, dining room, eat-in kitchen, and hardwood floors throughout.

Street parking available. Close to #33 bus line and interstate on-ramp; walking distance to shopping and Elmwood High School.

$1,400/month, utilities included. Pets okay. Call 312.555.5555.

Rental Listing Booklets

There are national, regional, and local publications that advertise rental properties—particularly for major metropolitan areas. These free guides—*Apartment Guide* and *For Rent,* two of the nationals—are available in supermarkets and other places of business. They are mostly used by large rental companies, but they do offer ad space to "the little guy."

Check your area for a local version by contacting your local landlord association or by browsing area convenience stores. Next, find out if advertising in the guide is cost effective. Generally, advertising in these guides is more expensive than running classified ads in the newspapers, but depending on your area, it may be worthwhile to try it.

List with a Rental Agent

There are plenty of companies and agents out there who are willing to take on the responsibility of marketing your property and finding you a tenant. Many real estate agents will handle rentals as a side job. Keep in mind that either you pay them for the service or the tenant does. That said, here are some pros and cons of working with a rental agent:

Pros

- ◆ They will do all the work—including making the decisions on how and where to advertise.
- ◆ They are likely to find higher-end tenants—especially if the tenant is paying the agency's fee.
- ◆ Rental agents and agencies are a good way to open your marketing to people who are relocating to your town or neighborhood.
- ◆ You do not have to pay until they find you a tenant.

Cons

- ◆ They may spend a lot of your money on advertising if your contract does not specify what costs are included in their rental service.
- ◆ If you pay the fee, it could cost you the equivalent of one month's rent.
- ◆ These relocators may not be likely to rent long term.
- ◆ They may take a while to find a tenant—and meanwhile, you are losing money!

Target Good Tenants

Whichever means you use to market your rental property, keep an eye on your target market: responsible, financially stable, long-term tenants. You want to position your property to appeal to these people by stressing the quality of the property, its cleanliness, and its upkeep.

Price also has a lot to do with who you attract. If you accidentally undervalue your property and offer an unusually low rent, you may attract people who cannot afford the real price, which you will eventually want to charge once you wise up. But do not be afraid to slightly overvalue the property to see if you can get a nibble from a good tenant.

And finally, where you advertise helps target the population you are advertising to. Advice involving letting locals know about your property should be taken with a grain of salt if your property is in a declining neighborhood. You might do better to target slightly wealthier communities.

Do Not Discriminate

It is illegal for you as a landlord to discriminate against any particular group or person when making a decision to rent. The 1988 Federal Fair Housing Act ensures that landlords cannot discriminate based on race, color, national origin or ancestry, religion, sex, familial status, or physical disability.

Be careful that you do not include any hint of discrimination in your advertising. Avoid describing the type of tenant you are looking for to keep from getting into legal trouble.

Examples

- ◆ Do not include "no children, please" in your classified ad.
- ◆ Do not suggest that your one-bedroom is great for singles.
- ◆ Do not point out that your rental house is a quick drive to the church or steps from the synagogue.

Show the Property

Your advertising is in place. You have the word-of-mouth grapevine humming with news of your rental; your classified ads are placed; your signs are up; and your flyers have been distributed and posted on bulletin boards. What happens next? If your advertising works and your timing is good, then your phone will start ringing off the hook. Your job then is to begin the screening process and nudge all promising callers to come and see your property for themselves.

Most landlords would agree that taking calls from prospective tenants and showing the property is the most time-consuming aspect of the business. So, when you start to advertise a vacancy, clear your schedule. Set aside time to talk to callers, whether they end up scheduling an appointment or not; plus travel time to the property if you do not live on the premises; plus waiting-around time while you sit there waiting for latecomers and no-shows.

Man the Phones

If you do a good job with your advertising, you should start getting phone calls within a day or two. If you do a great job, the rental market is tight, or your property is simply outstanding, you are going to get a lot of calls. If you find that you are overwhelmed with the quantity of phone calls you are getting or most callers want to know simple facts like if you allow dogs or if utilities are included in the rent, then you should consider screening initial calls with your answering machine or voice mail. Here is how it works:

1. Record a greeting message that includes basic information about your property. Tell callers more than you did in your ad or flyer and be sure to address any questions you have already heard.

2. Callers who have three Great Danes will hang up when they hear no dogs on your message, saving time for both of you.

3. Return any phone messages as promptly as possible. Callers are probably working their way down a list of possible properties, and you want to reach them before they are on their way to becoming someone else's tenant.

Example

Hello, this is Bob. If you are calling about the house for rent, please listen carefully. It is a three-bedroom house on Swing St. and has a living room, dining room, eat-in kitchen, one and a half baths, and a full basement. There is a two-car garage and a back deck. The rent is $1,500 a month plus all utilities except water. No pets are allowed. Leave a message if you are interested, and I will call you back within two business days. Thanks for calling.

When you answer the phone in person (or when you return a prospect's call) be ready to talk about the property and answer questions. If you are in a noisy environment, negotiating heavy traffic, or in the middle of an important meeting, do not answer your phone. Listen to the message and return the call as soon as you are in a more appropriate place and can give the prospect your full attention. You want to sound competent and professional, not scattered and untrustworthy.

At Your Fingertips

When you're advertising rental property, make sure you have these items in front of you every time you answer the phone:

- A cheat sheet on the property—especially if you are showing more than one place or this is your first time showing this property
- Directions to the rental from north, south, east, and west, including public transportation, so you are ready to tell them how to meet you there for the showing
- Your personal calendar so you can make an appointment without creating a conflict

Full-Time Worker, Part-Time Landlord

If you have a job that prevents you from taking calls for your landlording business during the day, here is how to handle the flood of phone calls: Record a greeting saying you are unable to take their call right now, but will return the call after 5:00 PM—or whatever is appropriate. That way your tenants or possible tenants will not be frustrated at not hearing back from you quickly.

Once you are on the phone with the caller, give him or her a chance to ask questions about the property first. This can save you both valuable time. Also, use this as an opportunity to point out some more good features and sell, sell, sell.

If your answers do not send them packing, then it is your turn. This first phone conversation is actually your first chance to screen your possible tenants. Find out who would be moving in (A family? Roommates? A football team?), where they live now, when their current lease is up, and their financial state. The most diplomatic way to handle the financial question is to tell them what you will require up front.

Example

As my ad says, the rent is $1,500 a month, and I require the first and last month in advance, plus a $1,000 security deposit. If you end up taking the place, would you be able to have that money by the first of October?

Take notes on your conversation so that you can keep all your prospects straight. If the tenant is still interested after this exchange, ask if she wants to see the place. If she hesitates, do not press the subject. You are likely to end up standing around waiting and she will never show. Instead, ask if she has any other questions or concerns. If not, and she still does not want to meet, suggest that she call you back when she is ready.

Landlord Question and Answer

Here are some questions you should be prepared to answer about your rental property:

- Do you allow pets?
- Is the property nonsmoking?
- How much is the pet deposit?
- Are utilities included?
- What are the average utility bills?
- Is there parking?
- Is it close to public transportation?
- Does the property have a washer and dryer? How much does it cost?
- Is there a dishwasher?
- What is the square footage of the apartment/house?
- When is the rent due?
- Can I get cable/satellite there?
- Can I get Internet access?
- When can I move in? Can I move in early?

Here are some questions you should ask interested prospects before you arrange to meet in person:

- What date are you looking to move?
- How many people would be moving in? Do you have any roommates?
- The rent is $1,500 a month. Is that in your price range?
- Where are you living now? Why are you moving?
- Do you have any pets?
- Do you or your roommates/family members smoke?

Schedule the Showings

If the caller wants to see the property, consult your calendar and schedule a time that works for both of you. Typically this will be in the evening or during the weekend.

IMPORTANT NOTE

Your property will look best in daylight. If possible, try to schedule the appointment at least half an hour before sundown.

Ask for the caller's phone number in case you have to reschedule. (Do not actually reschedule. This is a tactic to ensure that he or she feels obligated to actually show up for the appointment.)

Also, be specific about where you will meet. Will you be inside the property or waiting outside? Let them know so he or she will feel more confident about the meeting.

IMPORTANT NOTE

This first phone call is when you will set the tone for the landlord-tenant relationship. Try to strike a balance between firm and friendly, professional and relaxed. Treat it like a job interview—but you are both the interviewer and the one being interviewed.

When it is time to meet the prospect at your rental property, come ready for action. You should have:

◆ Your notes from the phone conversation so you remember who this person is
◆ Several copies of the rental application
◆ Pencils or pens
◆ Copies of your policies to review with very interested people
◆ Your cell phone

Then, follow these steps for each showing:

1. Show up a bit early if you can. This puts you in a slight position of power and may give you more time to scope out the prospect(s) as they arrive. Also, if the property is vacant, you can do a quick walk through to make sure it is clean and ready to show.

2. When the prospect(s) show up, welcome them, and introduce yourself. (Keep in mind that they probably did not take notes on the phone call and may not remember your name.)

3. Briefly show them around the outside of the property first, then lead them inside.

4. It is a good idea to walk them through all the rooms once and point out features such as good water pressure, new windows, any storage, kitchen appliances, plenty of electrical outlets, and so on. Be sure to mention any work done in the past year.

5. Once the guided tour is over—and it should be brief—ask if they have any questions for you. If not, suggest they take more time to look around and make yourself scarce. Go examine the outside hall for cobwebs or check your voice mail messages in the room they are least likely to examine in detail.

6. Once they have had time to examine everything they are interested in, offer an open-ended question, such as, "So...what do you think?" This allows time for more questions, an easy out, or even a "We'll take it!"

7. Gauge their reaction to the property, and if they seem interested, offer them an application.

8. If they take it, ask for a photo ID to verify their name, address, and any other information you will need. This is probably the last time you will see them in person before you check their credit and references and you want to make sure you are checking out the right people.

9. If they are interested enough to take an application, this is the time to go over any restrictive policies they should know about. Mention limitations on pets, smoking, number of occupants, and so on. Any of these may be an instant disqualifier. If no red flags are raised by your rules, give them a list of all your policies along with the application so they can read it over.

10. Explain that you will perform a credit check and check references once they turn in the application, and also what money is due to seal the agreement. Make sure they understand how much money they will need and what date they will need it—most people need a little advance warning to come up with that much money.

If a prospect is very interested in the property, consider asking for a deposit and completed application on the spot. Of course, you will still thoroughly check his references and credit, but the deposit ensures that you will not rent to anyone else while his application is in process. And, for the record: This process should only take a couple of days. Check out his credit and so on immediately. If for some reason he does not pass your examination, return his deposit with an explanation. If he decides he does not want to rent from you, you get to keep the deposit.

If a prospect tries to negotiate rent or rental terms, stand firm. It is best to stick to the pricing terms and policies you originally set. Once you start negotiating terms, you are on a slippery slope to less rent and potentially more work for you.

Safety Issues

When you are showing your rental property, keep in mind that you are making arrangements to meet strangers you know nothing about (who knows if what they tell you over the phone is true?) all by yourself in an empty house or apartment. It does not hurt to take precautions to protect yourself.

Basic Safety Measures

- If a prospect were to commit a crime, they would most likely rob you. Do not carry valuables to showings. That includes cash, expensive jewelry, fur, or leather coats. And if your property is empty, do not keep anything of value in it.
- Tell a family member or friend the time of each appointment and who you are meeting. Give the prospect's name and phone number.

Going a Step Further

- Check the person's name and number before you meet. Call her back at the number she gave you to confirm that she can be reached there.
- If you are nervous about meeting strangers alone, bring a friend along. But keep in mind that your prospective tenant may be nervous about her own safety.
- Alternatively, call a designated friend on your cell phone as soon as you see the prospect approach. Tell him you will call him back—within earshot of the prospect.

(continued)

Safety Issues (*Continued*)

If You Are Really Nervous

- ◆ Ask to see the person's photo ID when you meet him to make sure he is who he says he is. *Then,* call your designated friend and give him the person's name.
- ◆ Carry a noise-making panic button or whistle.

It is up to you to gauge how careful you should be. Determining factors include where your property is located, how remote it is, and how physically vulnerable you are.

As you can see, a lot goes into the task of marketing your rental vacancies and filling them with suitable tenants. In the next section, we'll show you how to set rents and structure leases—two more important elements that must be addressed before you can start achieving success as a property manager.

CHAPTER 9

Setting Rents and Structuring Leases

One of the most important decisions you will make as a new property manager is how much rent to charge for your property. If you have bought an existing rental property, this decision will not be required until a tenant's lease is up, but if you are starting from scratch, you need to set a figure before you can advertise and fill your first vacancy.

High Rent versus Low Rent

The problem with setting your monthly rent too high is that you can end up increasing the length of time your rental property is vacant—and that can add up to a substantial loss of funds—more than if you were to charge and get a lower rent. The problem with setting your rent too low is that while you are likely to get a tenant right away, you will basically lose money every month. If your rent is $50 lower than comparable properties on the market, then that is $600 a year that you could have put in your bank account. Think how far that money would go toward helping with your landlording expenses.

Calculating How Much Rent to Charge

You may feel that you can set the rent at whatever amount you want. But like most things, rent is driven by the market. Of course, it is always good to know how much money you are going to make—or lose—but ultimately, the amount of rent you charge must be determined by supply and demand.

Here are the steps you should take in determining rent.

1. Figure Your Property Management Expenses

This includes your mortgage payment on the property, insurance, utilities, cost of hiring an accountant and/or property management help, plus maintenance and repairs, along with any office expenses you have. Estimate a year's worth of these expenses or base this total on last year's income tax papers. Divide your annual expenses by 12 to find out how much rent you will need each month to break even. Of course, your rent should be higher than this so that you make a profit—but do not use this figure to set your rent. Simply use it as a point of reference to see how successful you will be.

2. Check Your Local Rental Market

What are other landlords charging for comparable properties? The easiest way to research this is to read through your local classified ads for rentals or to drive around your town or neighborhood looking for For Rent signs. Then, check the prices. Make sure the property you are checking is similar to your own. Not all three-bedroom houses are alike. Note the number of rooms, amenities, neighborhood or school district, and so on to find those closest to what you offer. You may want to call the phone number on the sign or from the ad and speak with the landlord. You may even go see the property. If this is the case, be honest about your status as a rental owner—and be sure to return the favor some day. You can also check with your local landlords association to see if information on comparable rents is available or talk to other landlords about their rents. If a similar apartment seems to be priced too high, ask how long it has been on the market. Remember, you are looking at the rents charged for properties that are currently vacant and for rent, not occupied properties. There may be a difference between the two, and you are targeting the competition—meaning the apartments or houses that your prospective tenants are comparing with yours.

> ### Landlord Insights
>
> Because I am not in town to take care of things, I make the rent a little cheaper because the tenants will have to take a little more responsibility.
> —Paul Lorenz, long-distance landlord, Paducah, Kentucky

3. Estimate Your Own Rent

 Once you have an idea of how much comparable properties in your area are renting for, price your own rental accordingly. When in doubt, set your rent at the higher end of the scale and see if you get any takers. You will hear comments from prospective tenants if they think your rent is unfair, and if you do not get any nibbles in a week or so, lower the price. Do not negotiate with anyone about your advertised rent—you might be seen as wishy-washy and open to negotiation on everything.

IMPORTANT TIP

Even if you end up hiring a property management company to handle your rentals, you should go through these steps. You became a landlord for the additional income, and you will want to make sure you are getting the appropriate amount of rent each month.

Increasing the Value of Your Rental

There are ways to get more rent out of a tight market—or any market for that matter. If you increase the value of your rental property, you can justify charging a higher monthly rent, and you are more likely to get it, too. Here are some ways you can boost the value of the property:

- ◆ Include parking.
- ◆ Install a washer and/or dryer or make them available in a multi-unit building.
- ◆ Install infrastructure for cable, satellite TV, and/or DSL Internet service.
- ◆ Install a security system.
- ◆ Install air conditioner(s).
- ◆ Redecorate—sand floors or add new carpet.

- Add a hot tub, swimming pool, or a deck.
- Allow pets.

Some of these steps are quite expensive; it is up to you to determine if the costs of improving your property can justify the increased rents.

When, Why, and How to Lower Rent

It is sad but true—there may come a time when you have to lower the rents you previously set. If the rental market is flooded with property and renters can pick and choose the best home, you may have to bring your price down to attract good tenants—but it is likely that other landlords will be doing the same. You should be able to tell quickly if your rents need to come down, because you will not attract any applicants for your property, let alone tenants.

Do your research to see what the market is doing and talk to other landlords to get a feel for a fluctuating situation. If things are changing fast, this may be a good time to switch from a yearlong lease to a 6-month lease or even a month-by-month lease, so that you are not locked into a low rent situation for 12 months.

A Final Word on Rents

You can see that it is a good idea to stay tuned in to what is happening in your local rental market. Keeping an eye on rents, number and types of properties available, and other fluctuations gives you direct input into the perceived value of your rental property. Joining a local landlords association can help you stay informed and may give you more information than you can get on your own. Otherwise, check your classified ads regularly to see what is happening in your area.

Structuring Leases

As a property manager, your lease or rental agreement is extremely important. It is a legal contract that binds your tenant (and you) to specifics including payment of rent, use of property, and penalties for late payment and other problems. It is your protection against a lawsuit, and it will further protect you if you are hauled in to court. It also contains your official policies and house rules, which protect your interests and your property.

Rental Agreements and Leases

You will find the following forms on www.completelandlord.com:

- ◆ Residential Lease (Form LF310)
- ◆ Monthly Rental Agreement (Form LF255)
- ◆ Lease with Purchase Option (Form LF237)

You should put thought and care into your official lease and continue to update and add to it as you learn from your experiences. You can start with a standard lease template like the one found on www.completelandlord.com, and you may tailor it to a specific property. You can add a clause about lawn care on the lease you use for the single-family home or add a stricter policy on noise for a multiunit building.

IMPORTANT NOTE

Your state and county laws—and even city laws—may dictate certain policies, rents, and other major factors. Make sure you are using a lease template that is specific to your state and local laws. (Many state-specific leases are available on www.completelandlord.com.) When in doubt, have an attorney look over your final draft.

Types of Agreements

As the landlord, you can set up a rental agreement for any time frame you like. Typically, leases are for one year, but you can write a six-month lease, a nine-month lease—whatever you prefer. Of course, prospective tenants might find such an agreement a bit unusual, but more importantly, really good tenants—the reliable, pay-on-time type—are most likely looking for a year commitment.

If you do not want to commit to a year, you can offer a month-to-month rental agreement. This type of agreement is as legally binding as a lease, but either party can get out of the contract with 30 days notice. If you rent to a new tenant with a month-to-month agreement starting May 1, they can tell you on August 1 that they are moving at the end of the month, and you will have to let them go and start looking for new tenants. Similarly, on August 1 you can tell them to get out at the end of August if you want to.

Lease-to-Buy Arrangements

If you are willing to sell a rental property, you can offer a lease-to-buy agreement (also known as an option to purchase), which allows a tenant to rent the property that they ultimately plan to buy. This type of arrangement would include a standard rental lease along with a separate legal document that offers the tenant the option of buying the rental property during a specific time frame—typically a year. The price of the property is listed in the contract, and if the tenant buys the property, you must sell at that price. However, the tenant can decide not to buy at any time with no penalty.

Here is an example: You are renting out the one-bedroom condominium you lived in before you got married. You are considering selling the property, so when you get a new tenant, you ask if he might be interested in purchasing the condo at the end of his lease. He agrees to the terms and the fact that he is not obligated to make the purchase. He then signs a standard one-year lease, along with a lease-to-buy contract that states he has one year to purchase the condo at the fair market value of $100,000.

The tenant pays rent, which includes a monthly nonrefundable fee—outlined clearly in the lease-to-buy contract—which will be applied toward his down payment on the condo if he takes the option to buy. If he does not take the option—because he cannot make the down payment or changes his mind—you get to keep all the monthly fees. If he paid a $200 monthly fee toward the down payment for a year and still cannot make the down payment, you keep the $2,400 (12 months of $200 fees). If he is still interested in buying, you can extend the option for another year.

Warning: Do not extend the time frame on a lease-to-buy for too long; you may lock yourself into a price that ends up being below the average home price.

What a Rental Agreement Includes

Regardless of which type of rental agreement you decide to use, there are elements it must include for your own legal protection. You will find a lease and monthly rental agreement at www.completelandlord.com.

Use the agreement as is—assuming the one you choose conforms to your state laws—or add or delete clauses to suit your purposes.

However you decide to acquire your own agreement, it should contain specific sections. Chart 9.1 is a brief overview of those sections.

Section	What It Is	Why You Need It
Identifying information	The address of the rental property, the names of all tenants (including children), and the name of owner.	Of course this ensures the lease is legally enforceable, but this section specifically identifies who can live on the property. Any additional occupants may be grounds for eviction.
Occupancy and lease terms	The date the tenant takes occupancy and the date he or she will relinquish occupancy, the length of the lease, and the statement that tenant will use the property for residential purposes only.	Ensures lease period, and prohibits tenants from running a business on your property—imagine liability issues if someone were to open a daycare center on your rental property.
Rent terms	Amount of monthly rent, when it is due, how it should be paid (check or credit card AND by mail or in person), who the check should be made out to, whether utilities are included in payment, definition of late payment and any charges or penalties associated with late payment; same for returned checks.	Clarifies payment issues and ensures you are covered legally on issues such as late payments.
Inclusions	Specify what is included in rent, such as any utilities, a parking space or garage, and use of common facilities such as a swimming pool.	Anything not included in this section will be paid for separately and/or independently, such as coin-operated laundry on premises or off-site parking.
Alterations and painting	Any alterations the tenant wants to make to the property must be approved in advance by the landlord.	Prohibits major changes to your property without your approval.

Chart 9.1 Spending a Tenant's Security Deposit

Chart 9.1 (*Continued*)

Section	What It Is	Why You Need It
Responsibility for maintenance	Specify the tenant's responsibility for keeping the property in good condition.	This is the basis for collecting any security deposit to cover damage, undue wear and tear, or extreme mess.
Responsibility for damage	Specify the tenant's responsibility for any damage to the property and any fees or penalties for damages.	Ensures that tenant is responsible, financially or otherwise, for repairing any damage he or she caused.
Insurance	State what is protected by the landlord's insurance policy and note that this does not include the tenant's personal belongings.	Lets tenant know that he or she is responsible for insuring his or her own belongings.
Notice of termination	Note that tenant must give notice of intent to vacate, though this does not release him or her from the terms of the lease.	Reinforces terms of lease.
Subletting	Specify that tenant cannot sublet the property without advance approval from the landlord.	Prohibits a tenant from turning over your property to an unapproved person.
Abandonment	States that if tenant leaves property without notice, the landlord can collect any rental money owed.	Reinforces terms of lease.
Attorney's and legal services fees	States that if any legal action is required between the tenant and the landlord, then the "winning party" can have the other pay all attorney fees and legal costs.	May help you recover any losses in eviction or other legal action. Of course, if you lose the case, you must pay the tenant's legal costs.
Renter's insurance	States that tenant is responsible for buying renter's insurance to cover personal belongings.	May protect you from liability suits or save you money on insurance if tenant files certain claims with own insurance company.
Disclosures	Signature/initial sentences that confirm tenant has read all disclosures.	Ensures you have shared lead paint disclosure, Megan's Law disclosure, etc. Can also be used if you use an addendum to the agreement that outlines all policies and house rules.
Signatures	All parties—every adult tenant and the landlord—must sign the lease.	Ensures that all parties are liable for breaking any terms of the lease. This is especially important if you rent to roommates.

Your lease—or an addendum to the lease—should also include your official policies or house rules. This ensures that the policies (such as number of pets and noise restrictions) are legally enforceable. Policies are covered in the following chapter, so be sure to examine that information before you finalize your lease.

If you deviate from the lease template you use, it is a good idea to run your final draft past an attorney to make sure your additions and changes would hold up in court. Also, check your state and local laws every year or so to make sure your agreement covers any new regulations.

Right of Entry

Your lease should include information on the landlord's right of entry. You have the right to enter the property, but only with certain conditions—and sometimes outlined by state law. Of course, you can enter in a case of emergency, such as if water is pouring through the ceiling of the apartment below or the smoke detector is beeping and no one is home. Otherwise, you may enter as needed for repairs and maintenance, though you cannot come in just to check on your tenants.

Most state laws require that you provide advance notice to a tenant before entering—typically 24 hours. Your lease should state the terms of your right of entry, including the amount of advance notice you will give.

Signing the Lease

Make sure your lease conforms to local laws and clearly states your requirements for the tenant relationship. Your attorney should review the lease language every year to see if any changes should be made. Also, make sure you set a deadline for the signed lease to be returned with the security deposit.

The lease signing is a good time to review all rental policies with your new tenant. Provide a written copy of these policies, and make sure your tenants understand the logic behind the property rules and regulations.

Set Firm Boundaries with Problem Tenants and Late Payers

If your lease has set specific terms for dealing with late payments or disruptive behavior on the property, enforce those terms. It might not hurt to go over your planned conversation with your attorney before you confront your tenant.

Inspect Your Property Regularly

Check every square inch of each unit at least once every six months. There are limits; a tenant has a right to privacy. Some state laws allow landlords to enter to make health and safety inspections. However, in nearly all cases, the tenant must have notice that the landlord plans to enter or has entered the premises.

Now you know the lowdown on how to set rents and terms, structure leases and other contracts, and take the necessary precautions to protect yourself and your property now, and into the future. In the next chapter, you'll learn about one of the most important aspects of your job as property manager: screening tenants. You'll also learn that with the help of the technology developed in-house by the experts at CompleteLandlord.com, this aspect of your job can be both successful and painless at the same time.

CHAPTER 10

Screening Tenants: The War Is Won before It Is Ever Fought

When you take the time to screen tenants you make a huge investment in your property management venture. That's because tenants are the lifeblood of your business, and the wrong ones can quickly turn your job into a nightmare. Just as you would do your homework before investing in a property, you should do ample tenant screening *before* handing the keys of your abode over to anyone.

The Long and Short of It

Why is screening so important? For starters, there are a lot of things you will not know about your tenants until they have lived in your rental property. They may be slobs or amateur tuba players or nudists—a background check is not likely to turn up habits like these. But performing a thorough check of each applicant's employment, finances, and references can save you a world of grief.

> **Landlord Insights**
>
> **How to screen possible tenants a three-step process:**
>
> 1. Give them an application to fill out and send back (this shows motivation)
>
> *(continued)*

Landlord Insights (*Continued*)

2. Verify the information (this shows honesty).
3. Ask for a deposit check from a bank account (this shows the presence of funds and ability to maintain a checking account).

If they pass all three, you have a good tenant!

—Independent landlord

Just imagine how you would handle a situation where your tenant is living in your property and cannot or will not pay the rent. Could you still cover your mortgage and other expenses? How would you handle the stress? By taking the steps in this chapter and checking your applicant's history before either of you signs the lease sealing your relationship, you can greatly reduce the chances of this situation happening to you.

Discover the secrets smart landlords use to attract, screen, and choose quality tenants. Learn the easiest and most effective methods to find the best tenants with CompleteLandlord's "Attracting and Retaining Quality Tenants Kit." Learn more online at www.completelandlord .com/store/attracting-retaining-quality-tenants-kit.aspx.

 When is the best time to start the screening process? How about the minute you have a completed application in your hand! That applicant—and maybe others—will want to hear from you as soon as possible. As you will see from the information in this chapter, checking someone's background takes less than a day, so try to complete all your checks within two or three days. That means making any initial phone calls right away, in case it takes a day for someone to return your call.

Your Rental Application

You will find a Rental Credit Application form on www.completelandlord .com, along with a separate Tenant Reference Check Form and a Banking

Information Form. You can use these forms and revise them to suit your personal needs or you can create your own. However you decide to handle the form, your rental application should include the following fields:

Identification
Complete name of applicant
Date of birth
Social Security number
Current address
Home, work, and mobile phone numbers
Emergency contact information

Move-In Information
Number of people who will be living in rental property
Number of pets to live in rental property
Have you ever filed for bankruptcy?
Have you ever been served an eviction notice or asked to vacate?
Have you ever refused to pay rent?
How did you find out about this property?

Rental History
Length of time at current address
Name and phone number of landlord
Prior address (at least one)
Prior landlord's name and phone number

Employment Information
Name and address of employer
Contact name and phone
Length of employment

Financial Information
Bank name, address, and phone number
Checking account number
Savings account number
Personal references
Names, relationships, and phone numbers of three personal references

Only by checking all these areas, and performing a credit check, will you know if a prospective tenant can afford your rent, will care for your property, and will stay out of trouble. Later in this chapter, you will learn how to check all the facts and come up with a decision on the tenant's rental application.

Who Are They?

When you're going through the tenant screening process, consider whether the applicants are who they say they are. To make sure you don't get duped, request a photo ID and compare their face to that in the picture. Do this for each adult you are screening, and make a copy of the ID for your records. Ask for their ID when you hand over the blank application form or when they return the completed form to you. If they forgot their ID, tell them you cannot process the application until you see identification.

If you think this step is overly cautious, consider how simple it would be to cover up your terrible credit by giving a landlord the name and Social Security number of your sister, the pediatrician, who has never made a late payment in her life.

Signed Consent

It is important that people understand that you will be examining their finances and other extremely personal information. You would think that by providing all the contact numbers for their employer(s), bank(s), personal references, and so on that they would understand this. But they may not realize you will be contacting everyone directly or that you will perform a credit check on them. To keep everything legal, you should have them sign a statement saying they agree to let you check the information they provide and to let you perform a credit check.

You can provide a separate form or include this statement on your application, if there is room.

Above the signature line, add the following statement: "I authorize the verification of the information I have included on this form, as well as verification of my credit history, as they relate to my tenancy and to future rent collections."

This will ensure that the tenant who is turned down due to a bankruptcy or other credit snafu will not come back and sue you for checking his or her credit or bank history without consent.

Check Them Out

Now that you have a completed rental application and have verified the identities of all adults who will sign the lease, the next step is to review the application and make sure that all fields are filled in and legible. If any of the information is missing, give the prospect a call and ask them for it. Either they will provide the information or you will discover that it is no accident they did not provide a phone number for their current employer.

Some of your work will be making phone calls to speak with references, and some will be Internet-based. You may end up sending some letters or faxes requesting information as well. The first few screenings may take longer than you expected, but once you get the hang of it you'll be able to get it done more efficiently.

IMPORTANT NOTE

Keep all applications (approved or rejected) in a safe place. When you are ready to get rid of them, shred them before you throw them away.

Performing the Checks

If you belong to a local landlord association, find out if it can help with credit checks, employment and financial verification. Your association may offer these services or your membership may get you a discount on a company that can handle everything for you. This will not include phone calls, but may cover all the web-based research described next.

Here are the checks you should perform. Don't skip any steps—remember that your goal is to cover all of the bases to ensure an applicant has a perfect record.

Rental History

The only way you can verify a person's rental history is to check with current and previous landlords, but first you should verify those landlords themselves by looking them up in the phone book. A rental company (such as a management firm that runs a particular apartment building) should be listed in the phone book, but even an individual landlord (such as yourself) may have a listing in either the Yellow Pages or the white pages.

When doing your research, check whether the landlord's address matches the one on your form. You can also try finding previous landlords on the Internet by going to www.google.com and typing in the entire name in quotation marks, followed by the name of the town where the landlord is based. If these landlords have advertised rental properties on the Internet (including online newspapers), they are likely to show up online.

Once you have done your best to verify that both landlords are genuine, give each one a call to find out what they think of your prospective tenant. Realize that landlords may not tell you much, based on one of these two factors:

1. Landlords can be sued for slander if they badmouth their tenants to you. Yes, even if they call someone financially irresponsible or a dog kicker in a one-on-one phone conversation with you—that is slander.
2. Current landlords may be eager to get rid of a deadbeat tenant and might tell you that your prospective tenant is no trouble at all, hoping the tenant will finally leave their property and come live in yours.

There is not much you can do to get around these two information blockers, but you can verify the length of time the tenant has lived there and that he or she paid the rent (maybe). Consider it a good sign if the tenant has lived there for more than two years.

Another good question to ask your fellow landlord is, "Would you rent to them again?" If the landlord cannot reveal details for fear of being slapped with a lawsuit, he or she can still answer this with a resounding "no."

Finally, verify that the applicant has no history of evictions. If your local landlord association cannot help with this, you may need to contract with a private service. You can search the Internet for "eviction search" to find hundreds of companies that specialize in this; others combine eviction searches with credit checks, criminal background checks, and other services. Prices vary but should not be more than $10 for each search (on eviction only), and some companies require that you pay a one-time setup fee.

How Do You Choose a Trustworthy Screening Company?

One way to check the authenticity of one of these search firms is through the Better Business Bureau. Get the complete company name and address (if possible) off the search firm's web site, then visit www.bbb.org and enter the information. A company in good standing should have a Better Business Bureau listing with good customer comments.

Employment Information

Just as you did with the applicant's landlord references, check the authenticity of her employer. If there is anything that makes you suspicious about either the company or the contact that the applicant gave you, call them up and ask to speak to someone in the human resources department. This should ensure a more professional call than if you speak with the applicant's direct supervisor or anyone else they listed.

Ask the employer to verify the information on the form, including occupation and length of employment and, if they will tell you, the applicant's salary. You are not likely to get more information than that out of an employer, but if you feel you have an informal or chatty person on the line, you might dig for more information.

If the applicant says that she is self-employed, you should check her income. Because cash flow can be uneven for self-employed people, the best way to do this is to ask for copies of her income tax forms for the past two years, as well as three to six months worth of bank statements. Check her income to see if it is comparable to the annual salary needed to pay your rent. Be sure to look at the big picture. Some independent contractors may be paid $10,000 one month and nothing the next. With income like that, they should be able to pay the rent on time.

If the applicant notes that she is unemployed, do not write her off just yet. First, check her bank accounts. If she has a lot of money in her accounts, you could consider her as a prospective tenant. To protect yourself, you might request six months' rent in advance. If she does not have the funds to support herself for more than three months, or if she lied about her employment on the application, keep looking for a tenant.

If the tenant lists other sources of income such as alimony payments, Social Security, or sales commissions, ask for substantial records to back up the information.

Financial Information

Start the financial due diligence by calling the phone number the tenant provides for his or her bank (or look them up in the phone book) and explain what you are looking for. The bank will probably want your request in writing and may provide its own form. Depending on your location and circumstances, you can ask to come in and fill out the form on-site (make sure you have the application with you), fax it, or mail it in.

The bank will verify the current amount in each account. They may request a copy of the application or form with the applicant's signed authorization statement.

Personal References

It doesn't hurt to call each of the references an applicant provides. While it is very unlikely that people would provide a reference that does not speak highly of them, calling each of these people may give you some reassurance. Another good reason to call is to make sure the applicant gave you real names and phone numbers of references.

If you cannot reach a reference because he or she does not exist or the number is disconnected, something is fishy. If, on the other hand, you have three solid references, then you have three points of contact if your tenant turns out to be a nonpayer, does a disappearing act, or gets in trouble with the law.

Credit Report

There are several easy ways to get an individual's credit report (see Chart 10.1), and it's up to you to select the least expensive and most effective approach. As mentioned earlier, your landlord association may be able to do this for you. There are also a number of local agencies that will handle this service. Most services go through one of the top three national credit reporting agencies, which do not deal directly with independent landlords.

The big three credit reporting agencies are:

Equifax	**Experian**	**TransUnion**
www.equifax.com	www.experian.com	www.tuc.com
(800) 685-1111	(888) 397-3742	(800) 888-4213
P.O. Box 740241	P.O. Box 2002	P.O. Box 1000
Atlanta, GA 30374	Allen, TX 75013	Chester, PA 19022

Company	Cost	Time	Other Factors
Local credit bureau	Subscription fee plus $30 to $40 charge per person you have checked.	Within half a day.	You will need to fax in the application so the bureau can check that the applicant has given permission for the check. This is your best option if you do not have Internet access or prefer not to use the Web.
Web-based credit reporting agency	Online service including credit check, criminal background check, and eviction search typically costs $10 to $20 per search.	Some searches can be done instantly while you are still online. Others—typically less expensive—can be done within 1 day.	Be sure the online service you are dealing with is reputable. Read their Web site carefully and check them out with the Better Business Bureau.
Ask applicant to order his or her own report from one of three national agencies	Free for you; may cost the applicant a small fee but no more than the typical screening fee charged by landlords.	Your applicant may be able to find a free trial offer and pay nothing; otherwise he or she can order a report from any of the three major agencies for $9.	Make sure you see the complete and real report. Know what a credit report from each of these agencies looks like.

Chart 10.1 Options for Getting a Credit Report

Your Responsibility Regarding Bad Credit

If the applicant's credit report turns up something negative, and if you reject him as a result of that bad mark against him, then the law says you have to notify him of the bad report. The Fair Credit Reporting Act requires you to provide notice to the person, including the name, address, and phone number of the reporting credit agency (one of the three national agencies listed previously), a statement that the agency that supplied the report did not make the decision to reject him, and a notice of the person's right to dispute the accuracy or completeness of the information on his credit report, as well as his right to a free report from the agency within 60 days.

Criminal Background Check

Many credit bureaus and online services will include a criminal background check in their general tenant search. If this is included and does not cost much, go ahead and check it. Otherwise, consider skipping it. Here's why: Most states do not require landlords to check the criminal background of applicants, and some states will not allow landlords access to this information.

If you can get access to the records, which will include any convictions and sometimes arrests, keep in mind that state records are generally not up to date, comprehensive, or reliable.

Reasons You Can Legally Turn Down a Prospective Tenant

- Lied or misled on rental application
- Incomplete application
- Excessive debt
- Poor rental history
- Poor payment history
- Criminal history
- Landlord or personal reference(s) did not recommend them
- Income/finances indicates he or she cannot afford the rent

What to Do with the Data

Many sources will suggest that the amount of rent tenants pay should not exceed a certain percentage of their income—usually 25 or 30 percent. But other factors can throw off this equation. It is better to look at your applicants on a case-by-case basis.

Here is an example:

1. Use your calculator to go over the person's income and credit history.
2. Estimate his or her monthly income after taxes (including any extras like alimony or Social Security).
3. Subtract any existing monthly payments such as car payments or student loans.
4. Check the remaining amount. Is there enough money to pay the rent and still cover living expenses?
5. Remember, if you are renting to a couple or to roommates, it is best to divide the rent among them when you make your calculations.

Factors that might influence your decision include the amount of savings the person has in the bank and the number of late payments for credit cards, car loans, and so forth that show up on the credit report.

Who Pays for the Background Check?

No matter how you go about checking the information on the form, you're probably going to have to pay for it. You may consider these fees a cost of doing business, but it is okay to pass those costs on to the applicant as long as they are reasonable.

Decide which services you are going to use to check credit, eviction history, and so forth, and calculate how much each tenant screening will cost. Understand that it's not ethical or legal to charge for the time you spent checking references. Keep the screening fee as low as possible, and ask for it at the time the applicant turns in the completed application form.

Acting as a Reference

After completing your background check on all of your applicants, consider that you will one day be asked to give a reference for your tenants. Most likely, other landlords will call and ask you the same questions you have been asking. But you may also be asked to act as a reference for a tenant when he or she is applying for a new job.

In either case, consider the liability issues raised in the section on rental history. If your tenant is not good about paying or caring for the property, be careful about how much information you give or how you phrase it. Keep in mind that even comments made in a one-on-one phone call can be regarded as slander. Also keep in mind that CompleteLandlord offers a tried-and-tested approach to tenant screening that is both affordable and easy to use. Learn more at www .completelandlord.com.

Making the Selection

Now that you have shown your rental property, received several applications, and thoroughly checked employment, finances, credit, and backgrounds for all applicants, what is next? How do you decide who you will rent to—or more importantly, who you should not rent to? Some decisions may be obvious, but others are tougher. Let's start with the reasons you absolutely must reject someone.

An applicant should be immediately rejected if:

- She refuses to provide a piece of required information such as employment history or a current or previous landlord.
- You discover she has lied about any aspect of her background.
- She does not have sufficient proven income to pay the rent.

All other reasons are up to you to decide, based on your values, instincts, and experience.

Know the Warning Signs

What about the gray areas of a background check or credit history? Here are some warning signs to watch out for:

Know the Warning Signs (*Continued*)

◆ *Credit history shows late payments.* If a credit report reveals many late payments on credit cards, car loans, and so forth, you can probably expect your rent to be late as well. But check the frequency of the late payments, and the most recent history. If the problem does not appear in the past six months, it may no longer be a problem.

◆ *Credit history shows a lot of debt.* Is the applicant carrying thousands of dollars in credit card debt? Do not condemn him for the debt—this situation is very common. But consider that he has a lot of monthly payments to make. Check his income and bank balances to make sure he can afford his debt and your rent.

◆ *Bank records show low bank balance.* A low or nonexistent savings account coupled with a low balance in a checking account may mean the applicant is living month-to-month on her paychecks. Of course, she could also have all her money stashed in mutual funds, but her income should clarify that possibility. If you think your applicant has no financial cushion, consider dropping her from your A list.

◆ *Tenancy check shows applicant moved around a lot.* An applicant who has previously rented the same property for more than a year could be a good tenant. One who has rented the same place for many years—or has stayed in each of his past two rentals for several years each—is ideal. Take a careful look at someone who has lived a year or less in his current and past homes. Of course, there may be a good explanation for his moves, but that type of history warrants a careful conversation with the landlords—and perhaps the applicant as well.

◆ *Criminal background check reveals past convictions.* If a criminal background check turns up a past arrest or conviction, don't immediately discount the applicant. Factors to consider here include whether the person mentioned her criminal record to you first or if she waited for you to find out about it. Mentioning it first shows that she is honest about it and more likely to be a safe tenant. Also consider what crime was committed, how many convictions she has, and when her last conviction took place. You can consider giving a one-time offender a chance, but someone with multiple convictions would be a definite "no."

Choosing the Best

Now that you have your list whittled down to applicants who passed your background check with flying colors, how do you choose among them?

Landlord Insights

The two toughest things about being a landlord are finding the right property and making sure you have good tenants.
            —Mark Berlinski, owner of multiple rental properties
                                              in Chicago, Illinois

The fairest method would be to take the one who applied first. If you made any promises, or accepted a deposit from anyone, you should go with that choice or have a good explanation ready. If you did not take any deposits or make any promises regarding priority, then the choice is up to you. You can go with your gut instinct on someone or pick the person with the highest bank balance or income. But when you are making the decision, be careful not to discriminate against anyone.

The Fair Housing Act

You must be very careful when rejecting an applicant. If any discrimination is suspected, you may end up facing an expensive lawsuit. The Fair Housing Act (FHA), passed by Congress in 1968 and amended in 1988, protects people from discrimination from landlords and property managers. The FHA applies to all types of housing: public and private, including single-family homes, apartments, condominiums, mobile homes, and other dwellings. The law includes some exemptions. For example, it does not apply to a single-family house sold or rented by a private owner without the use of a real estate agent, provided that among other conditions, the owner does not own more than three single-family houses at any one time.

The FHA does not apply to rooms or units in a dwelling containing living quarters occupied, or intended to be occupied, by no more than four families living independently of each other if the owner occupies one of the living quarters. The U.S. Department of Housing and Urban Development states:

> Title VIII of the Civil Rights Act of 1968 (Fair Housing Act), as amended, prohibits discrimination in the sale, rental, and financing of dwellings, and in other housing-related transactions, based on race, color, national origin, religion, sex, familial status (including children under the age of 18 living with parents of legal custodians, pregnant women, and people securing custody of children under the age of 18), and handicap (disability).

Note that physical disabilities referenced in this act include chronic alcoholism, AIDS or AIDS-related complex, hearing or visual impairment, chronic mental illness, and mental retardation.

You can see that the FHA covers much more than racial discrimination. It means that you cannot reject an applicant because you do not want young children tearing up your property. It also means you cannot pass over the unmarried couple who applied because you do not approve of their living together.

The key is to carefully consider why you are choosing one applicant over another and to make sure you are making a fair and legal decision. Because their rights are protected by the FHA, it is a good idea to tell applicants why you are not renting to them. If they do not have a problem with credit or other background checks, this is where the first-come, first-served method may come in handy.

When "No Pets" Does Not Mean "No Pets"

If you have a no pets policy, you must make an exception for someone who requires the assistance of a guide dog or other assistance animal. If an applicant mentions that he needs such an animal, check for a medical prescription for a companion animal.

Keep a Paper Trail

Because of the risk of a discrimination lawsuit, it is a good practice to keep records of all applications and rejections for at least the last three years. If you have all the paperwork (including the original application, your notes from phone calls and meetings, and a copy of your written notice of denial) that proves that you turned someone down based on bad credit history (and not marital status), you will be in a much better position to field any accusations.

How to Notify the Chosen Applicant

Once you have chosen the best applicant, call that person and let him or her know the good news. During the call, you should cover the following:

- Remind him or her of the amount of rent and security deposit you will require immediately.
- Review your major policies (no pets, number of occupants, and so forth) that might be deterrents.
- Set up a time to meet and get the rental agreement or lease signed.

Only after you have the signed lease and 100 percent of the required rent and security deposit monies (including a check that's cleared the bank) should you begin letting the other applicants know that the property is rented.

How to Turn Someone Down

Because of the discrimination issues mentioned above, it is best to send a written notification to those applicants who did not make the cut. It would be nice to also give them a call as soon as you can to let them know your decision. Do not tell them anything not included in your written notice; this just gives them more time to look for another place to rent.

Your written notification can be the Notice of Denial Form located at www.completelandlord.com. If you prefer to create and use your own notice, it should include the following:

- The date you send the notice
- The applicant's name and address
- The legal reason you have decided not to rent to him or her

Keep the notice short and sweet, and retain a copy of it for your records.

Should You Accept a Co-Signer?

Once in a while you will come across a prospective tenant who asks if you will accept him if he provides a co-signer. Maybe the person is too young to have a credit history or maybe his credit history is checkered. If you consider accepting a co-signer on your lease, it must be with the following conditions:

- ◆ The co-signer has to complete your standard application and pay any fee you would normally charge.
- ◆ The co-signer is screened with the exact methods and standards used for tenant screening, including credit check, employment, finances—the works.
- ◆ After reviewing the co-signer's bank accounts and income, you need to verify that this person can afford to cover both his or her own living expenses and your rent, in the event that the tenant cannot.

If the tenant, the co-signer, and you all agree to these conditions, the arrangement should be safe and the lease terms will stand up in court. If your tenant lacks a sound background, but if you have a legally responsible co-signer who is personally responsible for covering any rental payments the tenant cannot make, the arrangement will be as solid as any lease with a regular tenant.

Make It Official

You have made your choice and the applicant (or applicants) is ready to sign on the dotted line. Before that happens, go over a few important points in person at a 15- to 30-minute meeting during which you will review the lease and have your new tenant sign it. If the rental property is empty, you can meet there or hold the meeting at your home office or somewhere public like a coffee shop.

During that meeting, sit down and review all your policies and house rules with the applicant. Make sure the applicant understands each of the points clearly. Ask if he or she has any questions. It is crucial that you do this before the lease is signed—imagine if you have a tenant signed up and you hear the awful words, "What do you mean, you do not accept pets?"

You can use your own judgment about how many of your policies you want to review; if you have a lot of them, you may end up sounding like the world's toughest landlord. If that is the case, have your policies ready in writing and give them to the applicant to read through. You should definitely mention the most important policies, which include:

◆ Number of occupants
◆ Pet policy—how many; what kind of animal
◆ Smoking
◆ Payment of rent

In addition to reviewing your policies and house rules, this meeting is the time to review any disclosures you must legally make to a new tenant, including:

Lead Paint Disclosure

If your property was built before 1978, federal law requires that you notify tenants of possible problems with lead paint. This includes providing them with any information about lead-based paint and/or lead-based paint hazards in your property; any available evaluation reports; and a copy of the Environmental Protection Agency's (EPA's) pamphlet, "Protect Your Family from Lead in Your Home." Complete information on this topic is available along with a disclosure form and a copy of the EPA's pamphlet at www.completelandlord.com.

Megan's Law Disclosure

The 1996 federal Megan's Law requires that a list of registered sex offenders be made available to the public. Some states have their own Megan's Law, which may require that law enforcement actively notify the public of the presence of registered sex offenders. While it is not specifically required that landlords provide information on known sex offenders to their tenants, you can cover all bases by letting your new tenants know that they can obtain a list of registered sex offenders from their local law enforcement agency.

Once you have reviewed some or all of your rental policies—and given the applicant a written list of policies to review—and made all disclosures you are legally required to make, ask your new tenant if he or she has any questions. Take time to provide as much information as you can, and view the meeting as a good time to get to know him or her a bit better and to start building a good relationship.

Once all questions have been answered, it is time to seal the deal. Have the applicant sign two copies of the rental agreement or lease. Give one to the new tenant for his or her records. Collect the rents and deposits you have requested and make plans for a move-in date and for turning over a set of keys—which will be after his or her check has cleared, of course. When you leave the meeting, both parties should be clear on what happens next and when the next contact will be. After that, your first stop should be the bank to deposit that check as soon as possible.

When You Inherit Tenants

If you purchase an occupied rental property, you should know the existing tenants come as a part of the deal. Many times newer landlords have told me they thought they had the right to immediately evict current tenants once they bought a property.

However, once the purchase occurs, new owners are legally bound by the terms of the tenants' existing rental agreement, including their rental rate until their current lease expires. Only after this date can you implement your own lease and rental rate.

As the new owner, you must decide if the inherited tenants are an asset to the property or a liability.

You can determine this by looking at several factors, including: (1) the condition of the units. An inspection will tell a lot about how tenants will treat your property in the future; (2) rent payment history. Ask the current landlord to show you rent-received dates for all tenants for the past six months; and (3) tenant correspondence files.

If the current landlord has done a good job documenting issues as they arise, a quick look through the tenant files will give you a snapshot of any problems you may be facing. You might also ask a few tenants if they know of any problems with fellow residents.

Once you have a clear picture of the tenants you will inherit, consider the overall pros and cons of buying an occupied rental property before you make your final decision:

Pros

♦ You do not have to launch an immediate search for tenants.
♦ You begin collecting rental income as soon as you take ownership.
♦ You have some time to adjust to property management before you begin the process of advertising, screening tenants, and signing new leases.
♦ You can implement your own lease as soon as each tenant's existing agreement is over and raise rents as necessary.

Cons

♦ You are stuck with the current tenants until the end of their lease.
♦ The rent may not be as high as you would like.
♦ If a problem arises, you have to address it within the terms of the existing lease.
♦ You may lose tenants who do not like the changes you put in place with a new lease.
♦ All things considered, if the investment property is a good one, it may be worth it to go ahead with the purchase even if you suspect a few problem tenants. After all, you will only be dealing with them for a year at most.

If you do decide to go forward with the purchase, we recommend taking pictures of all units prior to taking over the building. That way, you have documented proof of the condition of each unit in the event tenants claim the damage occurred prior to their moving in.

A final word about screening tenants: whether the tenants are new to your property or existing residents, you'll want to treat them with the respect that they deserve while extracting as much information as possible from them, all in the interest of making the best possible tenant selection. Using tools like Tenant Screening from CompleteLandlord.com, and some of your own intuition, you'll be equipped to make the right choices when it comes to tenant selection.

CHAPTER 11

The Mechanics of Rent Billing, Collection, and Reporting

Even before your tenants are in place—especially if they are "new" tenants—you'll want to have a system in place for billing and collecting rent. Throughout this exercise, keep the following in mind: as a property manager, your continual goal is to get the rent money into your checking account each month on time.

There are several ways to do this. You can offer several options if you like, but no matter how you decide to handle this, make sure you tell all new tenants—and put it in writing—how and when you expect their rent. Also, be sure to let them know what name they should make their checks out to.

Your collection options include:

◆ *Ask tenants to mail you a check.* This is the most common and easiest way to collect rent. You may need to allow an extra day or two for slow mail delivery, but otherwise it should be foolproof.

◆ *Ask tenants to drop off their check at your home or office.* If you live near your rental property, tenants may like this option—plus, there is no room for the check-is-in-the-mail excuse. Make sure you have a secure mailbox or place where they can leave checks if you are not in.

◆ *Collect the rent in person each month.* Coming to the tenants' homes for the rent is not very common anymore. Use this only if you have a tenant with poor payment habits. The upside is that it gives you an excuse to check out the state of your rental property.

◆ *Electronic transfer from their bank account to yours.* With a signed authorization form from your tenant, you can set up a system where the rent money is automatically transferred from their bank account to yours on the due date each month. This is ideal for both parties—no lag time, no postage, and no late payments—as long as the tenant has enough funds in his or her account.

◆ *Credit card payment.* You must get set up as a merchant to accept credit card payments, and you will be charged a small percentage (1 to 2 percent) of every transaction, but if you have tenants who have trouble paying their rent on time, this may provide a solution.

Security Deposits

When you sign new tenants, you should always collect security deposits before they move in. These deposits, typically equal to one to two month's rent, should be held until tenants move out. At that time, the money can be used for repairs and cleaning—otherwise it must be returned to the tenants.

When it comes to security deposits, every state has different laws, and even some cities and counties have unique laws. Your local landlord association should be able to familiarize you with applicable laws, or you can check with your state department of housing or real estate agent.

Laws specific to security deposits may include:

◆ Maximum limit allowed on deposit
◆ What type of bank account is used for deposit(s)
◆ Who keeps the interest generated by the account
◆ How soon you have to return the deposit after tenant moves out

Unlike the first and last month's rent and any fees due at the time of move-in, the security deposit always belongs to the tenant and should not be spent by the landlord. Even if your state law does not require it, it is a good idea to put all security deposits in a separate, interest-bearing bank account (such as a money market account).

That way, you will not accidentally spend the money, plus it helps ensure that it is not counted as income on your taxes. The money will sit there, untouched and accumulating interest for the duration of the tenant's occupancy. Even if the tenant causes damage to your property or misses a rent payment, the security deposit should not be used until after the tenant moves out.

IMPORTANT TIP

It is easy to set up a new savings account or money market account specifically for security deposits. Even if you do not have business accounts, your bank can set up a new personal account for you. Talk to the customer service department at the bank where you hold accounts about how to begin.

Getting the Deposit

What is an appropriate amount to ask for when collecting a security deposit? If allowed by your state law, an amount close to 1½ to two month's rent on the same property is ideal. This ensures that if the tenant uses the deposit as a last month's rent—something that should be prohibited in your lease—you still have some funds left to cover any legal expenses.

If you are required to ask for a deposit equaling no more than one month's rent, set the amount slightly below your rent. This prevents the tenant from using the security deposit as a last month's rent issue; if your tenant pays $700 a month and the security deposit is $675, he or she is less likely to equate the deposit to rent.

Assure your new tenant that you will return the security deposit in full, plus any interest, after he or she moves out. Review any reasons that you would keep all or part of the deposit. (These reasons are outlined next.) This should help soften the blow after turning over hundreds of dollars in addition to rent. Also, give him or her a separate receipt for the deposit money, which will help enforce the idea that you are just holding the money.

Make sure you have 100 percent of the required deposit before the tenant is allowed to move in—otherwise you may have to fight to get any money you are owed.

When You Can Keep the Deposit

State laws are very clear about security deposits, so be careful: examine—and document—why you are keeping part or all of any deposit. Here is an overview of the reasons you can and cannot spend a tenant's security deposit:

Security Deposits CAN Be Used for...	Security Deposits CANNOT Be Used for...
Repairing damage to property	Normal wear and tear on floors, walls, etc.
Cleaning a bad mess	Your own time cleaning the property
Missing items	

Rent Receipts

As part of your record-keeping process and insurance against losing a future lawsuit, always give out receipts for rent. You can write them from a receipt book (available at office supply stores) or print out a standard form from your computer. If you are collecting the rent in person, hand the receipt over immediately. If you're not, then mail it.

Landlord Insights

We offer a 1 percent early payment discount, rather than depend solely upon late pay penalties. Most tenants appreciate the opportunity to save the price of a meal out, and it encourages a positive, cooperative attitude in their minds. Generally, it enables me to deposit *all* rent checks on the 2nd of each month.

—Jim Sutro, independent landlord in Half Moon Bay, California

Sending rent receipts is also a good way to communicate with your tenants. Include in the correspondence any information they might need, like a heads up about upcoming repairs or even neighborhood news like a street cleaning schedule.

Setting and Enforcing Due Dates

No matter when a lease is signed or when the tenant moves in, you should ask that the rent be paid in advance on the first of each month. That means that September's rent is due on the first of September. This is important because:

- This is a very common practice and tenants should be used to it.
- It is easy to remember.
- If you have multiple rental properties, all rents will come in at the same time, making it easy to keep track of any late payments.
- It should coincide with your mortgage payment.

IMPORTANT NOTE

If tenants move in midmonth, charge prorated rent, or $\frac{1}{30}$ of their monthly rent for each day until the next month begins.

If you have a tenant who gets paid on the first of every month and requests extra time for his or her paycheck to clear, consider moving the due date. By offering to change the deadline, you will increase the likelihood of being paid on time. You can still keep your late fee structure—just change the dates on the lease to reflect the new date.

When is the rent late? Typically 10 days after the due date. This is a fair amount of time; no mail delivery, lack of stamps, illness, or travel can excuse a check that is 10 days late. Some states require mandatory grace periods, so check with your local landlords association or state department of housing.

Note that rent paid within this grace period is still late, and tenants who consistently pay after the first of the month, but within the grace period, can be reported to credit agencies as late payers.

Your lease or rental agreement should include a clause on late payments. This allows you to legally fine any tenant who is officially late with the rent. But the clause must define "late," and must specify the fine. These factors are yours to determine—again, keeping in mind that your state law may limit either.

Landlord Insights

When our tenants are timely on their payments for 12 consecutive months, we let them pick a store of their choice where we purchase a gift card equal to a half-month's rent. This makes us heroes to our tenants and keeps them very happy.

—Independent landlord

There are several ways to structure the fine. Typical late fees are $20 or $25, sometimes higher, or 4 to 6 percent of the monthly rent. That should be enough to provide an incentive for the tenant to pay on time. Another way to set late fees is to charge a daily fee so that the tenant has to pay (e.g., $5 each day until the check arrives). This provides the highest incentive to pay rent if not on time, then as soon as possible.

Dealing with Late Fees

There are three ways you can structure your late fees:

1. A flat fee for any rent paid 10 days or later after the due date—typically $20 to $25.
2. A flat percentage of the rent for any rent paid 10 days or later after the due date—typically 4 to 6 percent.
3. A daily fee, charged for each day the rent is late starting 10 days after the due date—typically $5 per day.

However you decide to handle late fees, be fair and consistent. If you charge a late fee one month, make sure you apply the same rules for all future months. If you charge one tenant for a late payment, make sure all tenants are charged for the same offense.

When, Why, and How to Increase Rent

As time goes by, you will need to raise your rents. Perhaps you need to cover the expenses of improving your property or keep up with the rising costs of repairs and services. It makes good business sense to increase your income over time.

The best time to raise rents is when you have tenant turnover. Here is how to go about handling this situation:

◆ Check with your tenants at least two months before their leases are up to see if they plan to renew for another year or move on. Get a commitment from them in writing at least one month out.

◆ When you know a tenant is considering leaving, go through the steps of checking comparable rents (as covered earlier in this chapter).

◆ Estimate how much you can increase rent (if at all).

◆ Advertise your upcoming vacancy with the new rent amount.

Raising Rents

Though never popular with tenants, rent increases are a necessary part of property management and are essential to your business success.

As expenses, such as property taxes, utilities, and maintenance costs, rise over time, so should your rent. Otherwise, you are subsidizing your tenants, which I believe is never a good business practice.

To determine how much the rent should be raised, do some simple research to determine the rent of comparable properties in your area. The rental market is self-regulating, and if your property is priced higher than comparable properties, your tenants may decide to move rather than pay your increase.

Once you have made the decision to increase rents, inform tenants as soon as possible in writing. I also recommend providing a brief explanation of why rents are going up. Perhaps you have made some improvements to the property or the unit. Painting an apartment, installing a ceiling fan, or redecorating an entryway can help justify a rent increase. You could also detail any rising costs, such as utilities or property taxes.

Use specific percentage increases when possible—property taxes went up 7 percent last year, utility bills climbed 15 percent, and so on.

Also, break down the rental increase to simple and understandable terms. If it is a $60-per-month increase, explain that you are raising the rent $2 a day, which totals $60 per month. Most tenants would not go through the hassle of moving to save just $2 a day.

Smaller increases of 5 to 10 percent each year are often better tolerated than a steep increase every few years. Your tenants will also come to expect a small annual rise in rent and may be less likely to object.

Plan to give tenants at least 45 days' notice before the new rate takes effect.

If you have a tenant who plans to stay on your property and renew the lease, follow these steps—if not every year, at least every two years:

1. Go through the process of finding comparable rents to see if an increase is in order.
2. Using the previous year's tax forms, review your annual expenses to check your profit. You can also use some of this information to justify the rent increase to your tenants.
3. Advise tenants two months in advance that you will be raising the rent. You may not have an exact amount yet, but you can let them know whether the increase will be the size of a cost-of-living adjustment or something more substantial.
4. Be prepared for complaints and threats to move. Handle these professionally, and point out that the cost of everything goes up and that you have to cover your expenses just as the tenant does.
5. One month in advance, let them know what the new rent will be. Give them written notice as well as verbal.

Unless you have inherited a rental property with rents that are too low, or if something major has happened in your area or on your property that justifies a major increase (like installing central air conditioning), raise your rent in reasonable increments. That means 10 percent or less each year. If you keep bumping up the amount a little every year or so, you are likely to stay in line with both the rental market and your expenses, and tenants should not complain too much about small increases.

Landlord Insights

I look at the market to set rents. But I might test it by advertising a property at about 5 percent higher than the market to see if I can get it. I will lower it if I do not get a lot of response.

—Mark Berlinski, owner of multiple rental properties,
Chicago, Illinois

IMPORTANT NOTE

Rent Control

If your rental property is in California, Maryland, New Jersey, New York, or Washington, DC, it may be subject to rent control laws that limit the setting of and increasing of rents. If you rent property in a city or area with rent control, get the most current copy of the Rent Control Ordinance and check all regulations.

Don't be afraid to reward your best tenants. If you have a good tenant who always pays on time, takes good care of your property, and does not cause any problems, consider giving them a break on rent increases. You may want to charge top-notch tenants a slightly less-than-average rent to encourage them to stay. You do not have to charge the same rent to all your tenants; you can give some a lower increase or none at all if you want them to stay where they are.

If you are using a month-to-month rental agreement instead of a yearlong lease, the steps outlined earlier still apply. If you are going to raise the rent, do it when it makes sense and does not appear random to your tenant: Resolve to raise rents only on the first of the year or on the anniversary of the tenant's move-in month.

IMPORTANT NOTE

When you increase the rent for an existing tenant, remember to get the difference from him or her to add to the last month's rent you collected when the original lease was signed.

When, Why, and How to Lower Rent

Unfortunately, there may come a time when you'll be forced to lower rent levels. If, for example, the rental market is flooded with property—with renters picking and choosing the best homes from a list of many options—you may have to bring your price down in order to attract good tenants. The good news is that other landlords are probably in the same boat, and you're not alone in your challenges.

You should be able to tell quickly if your rents need to come down: You will not attract any applicants for your property, let alone tenants. Conduct your research to see what the market is doing, and talk to other landlords to get a feel for a fluctuating situation. If things are changing fast, this may be a good time to switch from a yearlong lease to a 6-month lease, or even a month-by-month lease, so that you are not locked into a low rent for 12 months.

In the next chapter, we'll help you handle tenant relations and communications in a way that assures that your property management venture is as enjoyable as it is profitable. Here at CompleteLandlord.com we know that can't always be the case, but using this book and our expertise as your guide, we know you'll stay on the track to success.

CHAPTER 12

Tenant Relations, Communications, and Problems

Once you have tenants living in your rental property, it won't take long for you to determine if they are assets or liabilities. The most obvious thing you will watch for is if they pay their rent on time, but there are other good and bad traits that will help determine whether you will want to entice them to stay at the end of their lease.

Remember, showing your property can be the most time consuming aspect of landlording, and if you can avoid that process, along with the expense of advertising every year, it is worth your while to court a good tenant to stay on for years and years.

Definition of a Good Tenant

A good tenant is, first and foremost, someone who pays the total amount of her rent promptly every month. After all, you are in this business to get rental money. But there is more to the ideal tenant than responsible payments. You want someone who:

◆ Takes good care of your property, whether she is fulfilling her obligations to mow the lawn or she makes sure to call you about maintenance issues before they get out of hand.

◆ Never causes neighbors to complain. You do not receive phone calls about loud parties, cars parked where they should not be, or police visits at 3 AM.

◆ Abides by your house rules and policies.
◆ Is interested and able to stay in your property for more than a year.

What You Can Do for Them

If you have tenants who fit all or most of these descriptions, you want to hang on to them! That means making them happy and giving them a reason to continue living in your property when their current lease expires. They are making your life pleasant, and here are some ways you can return the favor:

◆ *Keep their home in good repair.* Respond to any complaints and, if you do not hear from them, check in to see if anything needs fixing or updating. (Within reason, of course—stopping a dripping faucet is in order; replacing the bathroom vanity is not.)

◆ *Do not raise the rent too much.* When you talk to them about renewing their lease, a cost-of-living increase is okay, but do not drive away good tenants by trying to get more out of them. Save the big increases for when you switch tenants. Think of the money and effort you are saving by not advertising, showing, and screening!

◆ *Get rid of bad tenants.* If you have some noisy tenants living in the same building, do your best to bump them out at renewal time and assure your model tenants that things should be quieter.

◆ *Generally keep your property nice.* Do your job. Keep the exterior of the building looking good and the inside running smoothly.

◆ *Respect their privacy and rights.* Leave your good tenants alone unless they call you. Checking in every quarter or so is fine. And be sure to follow the law on letting them know when you need to enter their home.

◆ *Do not neglect the long-term tenant.* If you typically paint the interior of an apartment between tenants every year or so, offer to paint the apartment of someone who is staying for their second or third year. The same goes for updating appliances, replacing windows, and sanding floors or installing new carpeting.

Definition of a Difficult Tenant

In spite of your careful and thorough background checks, you may end up with a difficult tenant. Of course, the worst-case scenario is a tenant who pays his or her rent late, bounces checks, makes partial payments, or simply does not pay at all. This is a serious problem that may lead to serious action and even eviction, which is covered later in this chapter.

Hopefully, you will not have to deal with such a tenant. But other difficulties may arise, such as tenants who:

- Are overdemanding and request unrealistic amounts of work and effort on your part, such as repainting an apartment every six months.
- Damage your property, either by accident or on purpose.
- Draw complaints from neighbors about noise and disturbances.

What You Can Do about Difficult Tenants

Not all of these bad tenant traits should lead you to try to get rid of them. You can train people to become better tenants either by working with them or penalizing them. Here are some examples.

Overdemanding Tenant

When dealing with a tenant who calls you at all hours wanting immediate attention and repairs—be firm and focused. Do not jump to respond to every phone call. Instead, assure him that you will fix his problem the next time you are at the property, and do so in batch repairs. If the repairs he is requesting are too minor to consider, tell him so. Explain what your responsibilities are and what his are. A tenant like this can end up being an ideal tenant, because he can be meticulous in caring for your property. Other tips for dealing with overdemanding tenants:

- Set business hours for taking calls, along with an emergency number for overflowing toilets, and so on. Do not answer your landlord line after hours, though you can check messages to see what the person is calling about.
- Stick to your responsibilities as outlined in your rental agreement and policies. Point out the sections that cover repairs and maintenance to your tenant.

◆ If he asks you to make repairs or improvements not outlined in the agreement or policies, offer to have the work done if he will cover the cost.

◆ Offer to teach him how to handle a recurring minor problem such as a running toilet or loose doorknobs.

Property Damage

If a tenant damages your property, she is responsible for the cost of repairs. This should be clearly stated in your lease or rental agreement. You can ask her to have the damage fixed—or do it herself—and check to make sure everything is done to your satisfaction, or you can handle the repairs and present her with a bill. Of course, you have her security deposit, but spending that (or reserving it) before she moves out would leave you with no coverage for future damage.

IMPORTANT NOTE

If the damage is a safety hazard, like a broken lock on an outer door or a shattered window, have the repair made immediately and then present her with a bill.

Disturbances

As a landlord, you are not legally responsible for any complaints about loud parties, music, or domestic disturbances. If another tenant or a neighbor calls you about a noisy party late at night, advise him or her to call the police. But if the problem persists, ask the person complaining to send you a letter about the problem and start a file of written documentation, so you can substantiate the problem, if necessary.

If there is a recurring problem, send the problem tenant a note with a firm warning about breaking your house rules for noise, disturbance, and so on. Mention dates and times so that he or she knows you are aware of what is going on. Remind him or her that excessive noise, violence, and complaints from neighbors are all grounds for eviction.

Late Payer

If a tenant is ever late with his rent payment, call him immediately— a day or two after his payment is due—and ask him for it. Find out why it is late, and make a note of the reason for your records. In your conversation with the tenant, make it clear that the rent is due on time, with no exceptions. You want to ensure that he is not putting you at the bottom of his list of monthly bills, but rather at the top.

Each time you talk to someone about a late payment (or a partial one), you are working to enforce good payment habits. Hopefully it will not happen again—but if it does, call him again. Be firm and business-like and remind him of his obligation and that the lease requires that he pay his rent on time. Charge him a late fee if your lease includes provisions for doing so.

And, beginning with the second late payment, send him a written notice of late payment. Keep adding to that paper trail, because you may need it in the future!

Check Bouncer

If a tenant's rent check does not clear, ask him or her for a cashier's check or a money order for the rent immediately. If this happens a second time, tell him or her you cannot accept a personal check for rent anymore, but will require a cashier's check or money order each month—on time.

Handling Evictions

If you are stuck with a really terrible tenant—one who is not paying her rent, for example—then you need to get rid of her, no matter how many months are left on her lease. When you start thinking about eviction, first consider other options. Evictions can be messy and unpleasant as well as costly. Chances are that neither you nor your tenant wants to go through one.

Landlord Insights

I give an information letter to new tenants prior to occupancy. It provides them with my contact information and expectations. I provide them with the contact numbers for the various utilities that must be changed into their names immediately upon occupancy. I also like to remind them that they should change the batteries in the smoke detectors with each daylight savings time change and that it is their responsibility to change the furnace/air filters monthly when in use.

—Peter Martin, independent landlord

Legal Reasons to Evict

Can you terminate a lease and ask a tenant to move out immediately? Yes—if it is for a legal reason. Here are some causes for eviction that will stand up in court, as long as you have good records and a solid lease or policy statement:

◆ Failure to pay rent
◆ Late payment of rent more than once
◆ Repeated violation of a significant policy or house rule included in the lease
◆ Serious damage to your property
◆ Engaged in serious criminal activity on the premises, such as drug dealing

At this point, you can approach the problem tenant with some alternatives. Remember, your goal is to get her out of your property as quickly and painlessly as possible. Let her know you are willing to evict her—this should come as no surprise to her, since you should have been sending her warning notices and/or talking to her. Then offer one of these alternatives.

Negotiate a Voluntary Move-Out

Agree that she can walk away from some or all of her unpaid rent if she evacuates by a certain date. Get the terms in writing and have both parties sign it. You keep her security deposit, and in return, agree not to report her bad credit to a credit bureau or landlord association.

> **Landlord Insights**
>
> Be proactive. Not all tenants will have common sense or life experience.
> —Independent landlord

Cut a Deal

If you really want that tenant out, offer to pay for a moving van or even movers if she will leave. Or offer to hold her belongings in storage for a set time if she vacates immediately. If she is broke, this gives her the option to go live with friends or family for a while until she gets back on her feet—and you can rent your property to someone who pays!

Come up with your own deal. If you have a tenant who is not paying you rent, it is worth taking a loss to get her out of your property so you can start earning income again.

Things You Cannot Do

You want those tenants out of your rental house, and you want them out now. Do not lose your head—you do not want to do anything illegal. Here is a short list of things you cannot do to get rid of tenants:

◆ Lock them out—or in
◆ Pile their belongings in the street outside
◆ Turn off their utilities—even if they are in your name
◆ Threaten or intimidate them

Actions like these are dangerous and illegal in almost every state. And regardless of state law, you may be sued for everything from compensation for tenants' belongings to the costs of their temporary housing.

How to Legally Evict Someone

If you have tried everything and failed, it is time to start the eviction process. If this is your first time going through the process, you should hire an attorney to make sure you are doing everything correctly.

General Steps to Follow

1. Serve the tenant with a Notice to Pay Rent or Quit—in writing, of course. A notice is included at CompleteLandlord.com. This notice gives the tenant a short time (usually three or five days) to either pay the entire amount of rent he owes or get out. Most problems end here—if the tenant cannot pay, he will leave. If he does neither, then you start the legal eviction process. (If the problem is not rent but too many occupants for example, you would serve a Notice to Cure or Quit. In

this case, the tenant must solve the problem within the time frame by getting rid of the additional occupants.)

2. If the tenant pays the rent owed during the specified time, you must accept it. If he wants to pay after the time limit is up, do not accept any partial payments or the eviction process may be considered nullified.
3. File Unlawful Detainer (UD) action papers. (This is where your attorney comes in.)
4. Appear, when called, in court and get a judgment to collect the rent and an eviction.
5. Have the court serve your tenant with final eviction papers, including the date of eviction.
6. Have your local law enforcement agency evict the tenant on that date and give you possession of the property.
7. Change the locks on the property immediately to ensure the tenant cannot come back. Begin preparing the property for your next tenant.

If the eviction is uncontested by the tenant, this process should take between one and two months. There are specific time lines for each step, which is one reason that it is a good idea to have your lawyer handle this for you.

Landlord Insights

When you have to evict someone, find an attorney who only does evictions. He or she will be faster and have the ability to recover all your money. He or she will cost more, but it is worth it because he or she can get the tenant out faster.

—Catherine Brouwer, Blue River Properties, Memphis, Tennessee

IMPORTANT NOTE

Here's another reason to hire an attorney: Every state has its own detailed process for evictions, and some cities and towns also have eviction laws. While the previous steps are true across the board, the timing, forms, and other details should follow your state law.

Getting Your Money Back

If the court has ordered the tenant to pay you the rent they owe and you have not received a dime, you can hire a collection agency to help you get the money. An agency will charge you a hefty percentage of the funds they recover—as much as one-third or even one-half—but it is a simple way to get something out of that tenant.

Some credit bureaus will handle this task, or you can search for collection agencies in the Yellow Pages or on the Internet.

If you are a lucky landlord, and if you are careful about screening and selecting applicants, you will only need the beginning of this chapter (which covers keeping good tenants). But if you remember only one thing from the previous pages, it should be to keep careful and complete records. You do not have to be an unscrupulous landlord to be sued; good record keeping can help keep you out of trouble if a tenant should ever decide to take you to court for any reason.

Landlord Insights

I provide the tenants with a supply of prestamped envelopes, self-addressed to the landlord, 6 to 12 envelopes, according to the duration of lease. All they have to do is put the check in, seal, and it's ready to go. As I explain the procedure at the beginning of each tenancy, I've consistently received a positive reaction from each one. This gesture has been a win-win for both parties.

—Independent landlord

When Eviction Is Necessary

A successful landlord-tenant relationship is a two-way street—you need to find good tenants, of course, but it is equally important to be a good landlord who maintains a safe and comfortable property for renters, and who follows state and local laws on property management. Fail to do so, and you could face a rent strike or constructive eviction. In such circumstances, a tenant may legally withhold rent as long as you are not meeting the minimum standards in city housing codes.

The law requires the tenant first notify you of the unsafe and unhealthy conditions. If, after notification, you refuse to make repairs, the tenant can, in most states, legally withhold rent. (Some state laws prohibit the tenant from withholding rent to force repairs.)

Landlord Insights

After listening to a tenant's long story as to why he once again could not pay his rent on time, I simply asked if he would let me look at his birth certificate. He gave me a puzzled look and wanted to know why. I told him I wanted to make sure I wasn't listed as his mother because he was expecting me to take care of his problems like a mother.

—Independent landlord

A tenant may also enter into what is called constructive eviction, which occurs when the rental property becomes uninhabitable and the tenant can no longer live there. Typically, a constructive eviction occurs due to one or more of the following:

◆ Lack of heat, water, or electricity
◆ Failure of the landlord to maintain the premises, resulting in a breach of the warranty of habitability (expressed or implied)
◆ Repeated violation of a tenant's right to privacy by the landlord
◆ Breach of the covenant of quiet employment
◆ Substantial damage or destruction to the rental unit

Before a tenant moves out due to constructive eviction, he or she must notify you in writing of the problem resulting in the constructive eviction and give you a reasonable amount of time to cure the defects. If you do not, the tenant can move out and will no longer be held responsible for the rent.

If a tenant can prove that the uninhabitable living conditions were the result of action or inaction taken by you, and not a third party, and that she moved out of the rental premises within a reasonable time, she may be able to seek damages from you through the courts.

As a landlord, it is much easier to maintain your property, and keep good relationships with your tenants, than to deal with these preventable hassles.

The Eviction Process

An eviction order, also known as a writ of possession or writ of eject-ment, is an unfortunate part of property management for most of us at some point. It gives landlords the right to have a tenant physically re-moved from the rental premises and retake possession of the unit.

The good news is that landlords are not personally responsible for the task of carrying out the order because court orders are enforced by law enforcement personnel.

Landlord Insights

I discovered a simple method to work around the time delay when depos-iting questionable checks from chronically late tenants. Rather than wait the week or 10 business days that some banks take now to clear checks, I simply open an account at the bank that the problem tenant uses. Banks won't tell you the exact amount another depositor has in an account, but in my experience, they will check to see if there are sufficient funds in the account to cover the check you are about to deposit because it saves time and expense for both parties. (They will sometimes deposit the funds as cash, instantly available.) Still more time consuming than any landlord would like to deal with, but less wasted time overall, and no suspense about whether or not you have been paid or are being strung along.

—Paul V. Ames, independent landlord

Typically, a sheriff's deputy arrives at the premises with the writ of possession, orders the tenant to vacate immediately under threat of arrest, and seizes the tenant's possessions. The deputy stays until the tenant is completely moved out of the property.

Do not make the mistake of trying to bypass legal procedures by evicting a tenant without the proper court orders. You would be guilty of illegal self-help action, and the ramifications stemming from an illegal eviction are serious.

Work with a lawyer (or use an eviction service) to obtain a legal eviction order. Changing the locks, turning off utilities, entering the unit and removing the tenant's property, or threatening the tenant violates the law. The tenant has the right to sue for damages as a result of any of these actions. Play it smart and abide by your state and local laws.

Keep On Keepin' On

Ultimately, your goal will be to avoid as much legal wrangling as possible as a property manager, and to instead focus your efforts on finding those tenants who will pay you, care for your property, and stay put for multiple years. Finding this person isn't always easy. When you run into snags, just refer to this chapter for all of the help you need to get out of the jam and get your business moving in a positive direction.

SECTION FOUR

Getting Down to Business

13

Entity Formation and Asset Protection

The possibility of losing some or all of their hard-earned real estate investments is something most landlords do not want to consider. Unfortunately, the likelihood of this happening is real, and it can happen in unforeseen ways.

As a landlord, you face countless risks associated with property management and maintenance. Damage from lightning, fire, water, wind, and hail—not to mention personal injury claims from a tenant or even from visitors to your buildings—costs building owners and managers hundreds of millions of dollars each year.

How do you manage these risks without spending huge sums of money every year? How do you ensure that your own personal finances and property are protected? How do you make sure that you and your family or heirs are protected from unexpected losses? We wish we could give you solid answers to these and other questions, but we can't. What we *can* do is help guide you on the right path to managing these risks and balancing the cost-benefit equation in the most effective way possible. Ready to learn? Read on.

Step by Step

As a new or existing property manager, you'll want to use incorporating as your principal means of asset protection in the event of a lawsuit. The proper incorporation plan keeps personal assets (home, cars, savings, and investments) free from any claim should rental properties experience unreasonable and unexpected claims. The added tax benefits of incorporation are a bonus.

Next, you should establish a well-defined and cost-effective risk management program using these four steps:

1. Purchase a variety of insurance plans to reduce the risk of loss for specific perils.
2. Transfer a degree of risk to a third party (such as your tenant) by insisting that each tenant carry renter's insurance or sign Tenants Self-Insured Responsibility forms. For more information and help on renter's insurance, visit www.completelandlord.com to learn about the Minotaur Insurance Renter's Insurance Program for Landlords.
3. Retain some risks through higher deductible levels on your insurance policies to reduce premiums.
4. Practice good loss reduction strategies—keeping the building in good repair and leasing to quality tenants.

Managing Risk

Depending on whether or not you have employees, your property and casualty policy and general liability insurance coverage should include:

◆ A dwelling policy that will protect your property against: riot, civil commotion, vandalism, theft, glass breakage; lightning, wind, hail, volcanic eruption; fire, smoke, and explosion; and damage from impact by an automobile or airplane
◆ Liability coverage for tenant and guest injuries
◆ Crime policy and a fidelity bond to protect against employees and other burglary and theft
◆ Loss of rental income coverage

To reduce general liability insurance premiums, you should require a certificate of insurance from any contractor or repairman working on your rental properties. The certificate of insurance will give you proof that these contractors have adequate levels of liability insurance and are up-to-date on their workmen's compensation insurance. If they do not have adequate insurance, any damages become your liability and will increase both your risk exposure and insurance premiums.

As added insurance that your contractors will complete a job, require a surety bond that will allow you to hire another contractor to complete the work at the surety bonding company's expense should your contractor leave your job unfinished.

As part of your risk management program, use your CompleteLandlord lease rental agreement to require tenants to provide proof of renter's insurance coverage prior to taking possession and occupying the premises. Should you decide not to require renter's insurance, you and your tenants may initial the decline option to opt out of this requirement. Minotaur Insurance Agency provides easy access to a basic renter's insurance policy that is backed by an AM Best "A" rated national insurance underwriter and accepts all applicants.

Most renter's insurance policies provide coverage against everything from fire and theft to personal property and personal liability coverage for injuries and damages caused by tenant neglect. In essence, this provides an extra layer of liability protection for you as a landlord—and at no cost to you! An added benefit is the natural inclination of tenants to take greater care of your property when they are required to explicitly take responsibility for their actions.

Four Ways to Reduce Risks and Limit Personal Liability

Here are four ways to reduce your risks and limit your personal liability as a property manager:

1. Maintain adequate property and casualty and general liability insurance coverage on your rental property.

2. Use the CompleteLandlord Incorporation Kit to form a separate business entity to hold the title to your rental property with a separate corporation for each property to provide maximum protection. Talk to your accountant or lawyer to ensure you maintain a separate identity for the company in practice by not commingling funds and to learn about other easy-to-avoid traps.

3. Practice risk management techniques that reduce your risks and personal liability as a landlord such as requiring scheduled maintenance and inspections.

(*continued*)

> ### *Four Ways to Reduce Risks and Limit Personal Liability (Continued)*
>
> 4. Use the tools like those available on CompleteLandlord.com to screen prospective tenants for credit history, criminal background, eviction history, and other determining factors to ensure you only accept high-quality tenants.

Taking Responsibility

The landlord and tenant each have duties and responsibilities toward each other as well as duties to the property. Some of the duties are set out in the rental agreement. For example, the amount of rent the tenant must pay is a duty included in the agreement. Other duties can be found in federal and state laws—such as prohibiting discrimination in renting properties. State laws may require landlords to make specific repairs. A wide range of contract provisions and legal regulations cover your obligations as both a landlord and tenant.

> ### *One Landlord's Plight*
>
> In early 2008, a Manchester, New Hampshire, landlord was required to pay a penalty and take action to reduce the risk of lead poisoning at apartment buildings in Manchester and Antrim. This settled EPA claims that the landlord violated lead paint disclosure laws at certain rental properties in Manchester.
>
> Under the settlement, the landlord paid a $5,121 penalty and completed interior and exterior abatement work to address known or presumed lead-based paint hazards at properties she owns. This settlement is one of three significant enforcement actions announced in 2008 by the EPA regarding violation of lead paint disclosure laws.
>
> The violations were identified through an EPA investigation that began in August 2006, and they were alleged in a complaint filed by the EPA in June 2007. The EPA claimed that the owner did not comply with federal laws that require property owners, managers, and sellers to provide information about lead-based paint and paint hazards before the lease or sale of any housing built before 1978.
>
> Federal law requires that landlords and sellers who lease or sell housing built before 1978 comply with the following:

One Landlord's Plight (Continued)

- ◆ Provide a lead hazard information pamphlet that can help renters and buyers protect themselves from lead poisoning.
- ◆ Include lead notification language in sales and rental forms.
- ◆ Disclose any known lead-based paint and lead-based paint hazards in the housing and provide available reports to renters or buyers.
- ◆ Allow a lead inspection or risk assessment by home buyers.
- ◆ Maintain records of compliance with federal laws for a period of three years.

Infants and young children are especially vulnerable to lead paint exposure, which can cause intelligence quotient deficiencies, reading and learning disabilities, impaired hearing, reduced attention span, hyperactivity, and behavior problems. Pregnant women are also vulnerable because lead exposure before or during pregnancy can alter fetal development and cause miscarriages. Adults with high lead levels can suffer high blood pressure, nerve disorders, memory problems, and muscle and joint pain. Childhood lead exposure is a particularly acute problem for urban children of low-income families who live in older housing.

For more information see the following web sites:

- ◆ Lead paint health hazards (epa.gov/region1/eco/ne_lead/index .html)
- ◆ Lead-based paint disclosure rule (epa.gov/region1/enforcement/ leadpaint/index.html)

As you can see, there are many different landmines that can trip you up as a property manager. One of the best ways to avoid problems is by forming an entity that stands outside of your own personal assets to adequately protect your assets from the first day that you become a landlord. Take these steps and rely on the expertise of CompleteLandlord.com and you'll be in the best possible position to get down to business!

CHAPTER 14

Understanding Landlord-Tenant Law including Discrimination

Landlord-tenant law governs the rental of commercial and residential property and comprises mostly state statutory and common law. Put simply, these laws govern the legal relationship between a landlord and a tenant once they enter into a contract with one another.

In this chapter, we'll walk you through some of the basics of landlord-tenant law and help you avoid any pitfalls that may occur when either or both parties cross these legal boundaries.

Knowing Your Rights

According to landlord-tenant law, the tenant has a property interest in the land (your condo unit or single-family home, for example) for a set period of time. The length of the tenancy may be for a given period of time, for an indefinite period of time (renewable/cancelable on a month-to-month basis, for example), terminable at any time by either party (at will) or at sufferance if the agreement has been terminated and the tenant refuses to leave.

One State's Requirements

The Missouri Attorney General breaks down the requirements in this simple format:

One State's Requirements (Continued)

Tenants Should

- Pay rent on time.
- Use reasonable care and not damage property.
- Properly dispose of garbage.
- Refrain from taking on additional occupants or subleasing without the landlord's written permission.

Landlords Should

- Make property habitable before tenants move in.
- Make and pay for repairs due to ordinary wear and tear.
- Refrain from turning off a tenant's water, electricity, or gas.
- Provide written notice to tenants when ownership of the property is transferred to a new landlord.
- Not unlawfully discriminate.
- Put it in writing. (The best way to avoid later problems is to address issues in a lease. Put it in writing who has to mow the lawn, fix a clogged sink, or pay the utility bills.)

If the tenancy is yearly or periodic, then the tenant has the right to possess the land, to restrict others (including the landlord) from entering upon it, and to sublease or assign the property. The landlord-tenant agreement may eliminate or limit these rights. The landlord-tenant agreement is normally embodied in a lease. The lease, though not historically or strictly a contract, may be subject to concepts embodied in contract law.

IMPORTANT TIP

A common thread through all leases is the implied covenant of quiet enjoyment, which basically ensures the tenant that his or her possession will not be disturbed by someone with a superior legal title to the land including the landlord.

Unless the lease states otherwise there is an assumption that the tenant has a duty to pay rent. State statutes may provide for a reasonable rental value to be paid absent a rental price provision. Rent acceleration clauses that cause all the rent to become due if the tenant breaches a provision of the lease are common in both residential and commercial leases. Landlords are also restricted from evicting tenants in retaliation of action the tenant took in regards to enforcing a provision of the lease or applicable law.

Landlord Insights

A landlord with a lot of experience in our area tells tenants that he will walk the premises randomly with a police officer and drug-sniffing dogs.
—Tammy Rimbey, independent landlord

The Law and Advertising

Finally, federal law prohibits discrimination in housing and the rental market, with advertising being one of the most closely watched variables, which can be problematic for property managers. In your advertising, be specific in your description of the premises and provide the amount of monthly rent required so only those who can afford it will respond to the ad. If a security deposit and first and last month's rent are required, include that in your ad as well.

By making clear exactly what you are offering and requiring, you stand a better chance of getting a suitable tenant and avoiding possible problems in the future. For example, if you state in your ad that references from previous landlords are required, you automatically exclude applicants who are unable to supply such references.

Your advertisement should not and cannot in any way be considered discriminatory. Attempting to exclude applicants through advertising on the basis of race, ethnicity, national origin, gender, religion, or disability violates the Fair Housing Act. Local ordinances and regulations usually reemphasize these restrictions and may even broaden them. For example, the city of San Francisco prohibits discrimination in housing based on sexual orientation.

The Right Steps

Like any legal requirements, the landlord-tenant law can be confusing and difficult to adhere to, particularly if you've never dealt with property management in the past. Landlord-tenant disputes are a common occurrence in the renting process, and many could be avoided if both parties were aware of their rights and responsibilities. Approach the task early and ask your attorney about any areas you find confusing. Then you'll be better equipped to deal with whatever obstacles crop up down the road.

CHAPTER 15

Rental Property Finance

In Chapter 11, you learned about the mechanics of rent billing, collection, and reporting, but there's a whole other financial aspect of your property management business that can't be ignored: financial controls, reporting, and taxes. Without a good system for handling these elements of your business, you'll quickly find yourself up to your ears in paperwork, overdue bills, and sometimes, penalties and fines associated with late payments and related issues.

In this chapter, you'll learn the ropes of rental property finance as outlined by the experts at CompleteLandlord.com, who know all too well how challenging it can be to maintain a property management firm. By combining the information in this chapter with the resources available on the CompleteLandlord.com web site, you'll have a much better chance of running a successful landlording business now and well into the future.

Maintaining Records

Business owners don't like watching their filing cabinets overflow with old paper and documents, but that doesn't meant they can toss things into the circular file indiscriminately. If you are new to property management, the vast amount of paperwork that we, as landlords, encounter may be a little overwhelming. Even an experienced landlord can get frustrated with the paper trail needed for every tenant, business purchase, and financial transaction related to the job.

To play it safe, keep the following records both for tax purposes and to keep tabs on tenants:

- Tax records for the past seven years
- Maintenance schedules for all rental property organized by property and by type of work done
- Improvement schedules for all rental property organized by property and by type of completed project
- Building records, including original cost of the building, the mortgage, and information about when the building was constructed
- Bills, receipts, and invoices from all contractors, cleaning services, or companies that have done work on the rental property
- Insurance policies for all rental property (organized by building)
- Tenant contact information, including telephone number, cell number, and e-mail address
- Signed rental agreements and leases from all current tenants
- Financial information on disposition of all security deposits for current tenants
- Correspondence files with all letters, notices, legal actions, and contact with current and former tenants

These documents can either be maintained in a traditional filing system, or—if you are inclined to take one extra step to make your life a little easier in the long run—by scanning them and storing them on your computer. The key is to pick a system that works for you and stick with it. Try not to get hung up on whether your system is state-of-the-art or completely antiquated.

Taxing Matters

Property managers benefit from a number of tax deductions that can add up to substantial savings in taxes each year. Here are a few of the most common deductions that you'll be able to take:

- *Interest expenses:* You can deduct mortgage interest payments and interest on construction loans used to acquire or improve rental property. Credit card interest on expenditures for goods or services used in a rental activity is also deductible.

◆ *Property depreciation:* Residential rental property must be depreciated over 27.5 years.

◆ *Property repairs:* Your repair costs on rental property are fully deductible during the year they are made. Replacing broken windows, repairing lights, fixing floors, painting gutters, and other structural features are examples of repairs that can be deducted.

◆ *Local travel:* You can deduct the cost of any travel related to your rental activity. The IRS allows you the option of using the standard mileage rate deduction or actual expenses, which include vehicle repairs, upkeep, and gasoline. Choose the method you believe is most advantageous for your situation. The standard mileage deductions increase every few years, so ask your accountant for the latest one.

◆ *Out-of-town travel:* For any business-related travel to an out-of-town property, you can deduct airfare, hotel bills, meals, and other expenses. Remember to document these expenses carefully.

◆ *Insurance related to the rental business:* Fire, theft, liability, and flood insurance related to the rental property are possible deductions, along with health and workmen's compensation insurance.

◆ *Home office:* You may deduct home office expenses from your taxable income if you meet certain IRS requirements. This deduction may also apply to workshops or other workspace used exclusively for the rental business. As with all business deductions, check with your accountant for restrictions governing home offices.

◆ *Employees and independent contractors:* Any formal hires of full-time, part-time, or contract labor for your rental business can be deducted as an expense.

◆ *Casualty/theft losses:* If rental property is damaged or destroyed by a weather event or foul play, it is possible to get a tax deduction for all or part of the loss. However, this depends on how much property was destroyed and how much of the loss was covered by insurance.

◆ *Legal and professional services:* Fees to attorneys, accountants, property management companies, real estate investment advisors, and other property-related professionals can be deducted as operating expenses as long as they relate solely to rental activity.

♦ *Class fees and educational products:* The cost of taking real estate or landlord courses can be deducted. Even the cost of CompleteLandlord.com products or the cost of a Premium Membership can be deducted if you are a landlord.

If you hold property for rental purposes, you may be able to deduct your ordinary and necessary expenses (including depreciation) for managing, conserving, or maintaining the property while the property is vacant. However, you cannot deduct any loss of rental income for the period the property is vacant.

What Can I Deduct?

There are some rules governing your ability to deduct expenses as a landlord, and most of them have to do with how long you personally use your property each year.

You can deduct your ordinary and necessary expenses for managing, conserving, or maintaining rental property from the time you make it available for rent. Generally, there are two rules that would preclude you from deducting losses from vacant rental property: (1) You used the rental property as a home for more than the allowed time or (2) you used the home for a not-for-profit activity (as in, you didn't collect rents for its use). Other rules relating to rental real estate losses may preclude you from using the loss to offset nonrental income.

You use a dwelling unit as a home during the tax year if you use it for personal purposes for more than a certain amount of time. "Home" is considered personal use if used for greater than:

1. 14 days
2. 10 percent of the total days it is rented to others at a fair rental price

If your unit is vacant for the year or rented on the average of 90 days a year, you can use it up to 14 days for personal purposes. If you use the unit personally for 14 days or more, your deductions are basically limited to income. Any day that you spend working substantially full-time on repairs and maintenance (not improvement) of your property is not counted as a day of personal use. Don't count a day as personal use even if your friends and family use the property for recreational purposes on the same day.

IMPORTANT TIP

For more information about when you can and can't deduct expenses as a landlord, see the IRS publication 527 "Residential Rental Property" online at www.irs.gov/pub/irs-pdf/p527.pdf.

We could write an entire book on the basics of tax preparation for small business owners, but we'll leave that to the experts like Kiplinger, Intuit, and the Internal Revenue Service itself, all of which publish vast amounts of information about how to set up systems, comply with tax laws, and file promptly without fear of a potential audit. Check out some of these sites for more information:

The Internal Revenue Service

Small Business and Self-Employed One-Stop Resource

www.irs.gov/businesses/small/index.html

TurboTax Small Business Site

http://turbotax.intuit.com/small-business-taxes/

Kiplinger's Small Business Advice Center

www.kiplinger.com/business/smallbusiness/

Any or all of these sites can serve as good foundations for learning about the recent changes to tax codes, a listing of forms and publications that you'll need to file, and where to go for further help with your property management taxes.

CHAPTER 16

Insurance

The final—and maybe the most important—piece of your property management business puzzle is the insurance coverage that you'll obtain to keep your valued investment and those residing in it safe from harm.

As a residential rental property owner, you should be carrying the following four types of insurance coverage.

Property and Casualty Insurance

A property and casualty policy, in its most basic form, will provide you with protection against damage to your property from perils ranging from civil commotion, glass breakage, and vandalism to lightning, fire, smoke, or damage resulting from a car ramming into your building.

Hazards often not included are flood, earthquake, war, landslide, mudslide, or sinkhole. Depending on what part of the country you live in, you may need to buy separate insurance to cover some of these risks.

 If you keep personal belongings on-site at your rental property, such as tools, a lawn mower, or a snow blower, make sure your landlord's policy covers these things as well as the property. Also, your insurance may not cover the appliances in your rentals, so get a separate appliance policy, if necessary.

General Liability Insurance

This type of coverage insures you against claims by third parties (e.g., tenants or visitors) for negligence, damage caused to the property by a tenant or visitor to your property, injury to someone on the premises, or damage or harm to a third party who may be working on your property.

Flood or Water Damage Insurance

As the name implies, this coverage protects against any sort of water damage except sewer backup. Normally, this sort of coverage is in addition to a basic property insurance policy.

If you live on a flood plain, flood insurance can be expensive and hard to get. Consequently, people in areas susceptible to floods (or to hurricanes) must often rely on federal government-backed insurance programs to cover this sort of risk.

Umbrella Liability Insurance

For most businesses, this is coverage beyond what a basic liability insurance policy provides and comes into force after the basic policy has paid the maximum it will pay. In other words, this is insurance against an unexpected, even catastrophic, loss. A basic policy is sufficient only for basic needs and losses.

As you can see, the right kinds and the right amounts of insurance are needed to thoroughly protect you and your investment properties.

Speak to your insurance agent about any other types of coverage that you might need, as dictated by the area where you live or other variables. As you add new properties to your portfolio and grow your business, you'll want to keep that line of communication with your agent open, so as to ensure that you always have at least the minimum coverage required to recoup your investment in the event of a loss.

What Else Can You Add?

According to the Insurance Information Institute (www.iii.org), there are many types of coverage that can be added to the basic property insurance, including these common ones:

What Else Can You Add? (*Continued*)

- *Ordinance or law:* If a building is damaged by a covered cause of loss, this insurance pays for costs caused by the enforcement of any ordinance or law requiring demolition of the undamaged portion or for the increased cost of construction to rebuild with mandated construction materials.
- *Debris removal:* This coverage increases the basic limit of insurance (often $5,000) to cover the cost for debris removal necessitated by loss to a covered property.
- *Outdoor trees, shrubs, plants:* This covers the cost to replace landscaping plants lost as the result of a covered cause of loss.
- *Glass breakage:* This insurance covers the cost to replace plate and other glass, including cost of supporting bars or frames and cost of lettering and ornamentation.
- *Signs coverage:* This coverage insures electrical signs against many accidental causes of loss.
- *Boiler and machinery insurance:* This coverage pays for loss or damage resulting from accidents to pressure and refrigeration equipment, including boilers, air conditioning, and refrigerating equipment; mechanical objects; electrical objects; and turbine objects.
- Depending on the location of the insured property, it may be wise to add coverage for earthquake and/or flood.

Best Investment

As a landlord, your insurance policy may one day prove to be your best investment—or worst mistake, if you fail to get the right kind and amount of coverage. Here at CompleteLandlord.com, we tell other landlords, even if they are renting only one unit, they should switch from homeowner's insurance on the property to rental property insurance.

IMPORTANT TIP

Be sure to factor insurance costs into your initial business plan, as some states may command high premiums for coverage. In the Southeast, for example, insurance costs have shot through the roof in recent years, thanks to the slew of hurricanes that affected that area in 2004 and 2005. Do your research before you jump in so you don't get a nasty shock when the agent hands over a quote for coverage on your new property.

In general, a rental property policy provides the same coverage as homeowner's insurance, including damage to the building and to personal property, plus liability coverage for lawsuits, but rental property insurance also takes into account that the insured building or property is not occupied by the owner.

If you simply retain a homeowner's policy on property you are renting, you may run into trouble when you file a claim on your rental property. An insurance company can deny it because you do not have the right type of insurance for the damage.

Coverage can range from simple fire coverage to all-risk coverage.

How much rental property insurance is enough? Get enough insurance to protect the value of your property and assets, including short-term loss of income. Estimate how much equity you would lose if your building and everything in it were to burn to the ground—this is how much coverage you should have.

IMPORTANT NOTE

Encourage tenants to purchase renter's insurance to protect their belongings. A landlord's policy will not cover the loss of their personal property.

As you build your property management firm, you'll want to review your policies on at least an annual basis, and when any major changes (such as new acquisitions, or property sales) take place within your business. This will help you achieve peace of mind in knowing that your investment is protected and that you're not overpaying for insurance coverage that you don't need.

Special Topics

CHAPTER 17

Specialized Housing Markets

Just because you're getting into property management for the first time, or expanding an existing business, doesn't mean you're relegated to investing in a particular type of housing. A duplex located in a residential neighborhood may be a nice investment, but anyone looking to stretch their horizons a bit might find more satisfaction by purchasing and renting out a less traditional property.

In this chapter, we'll look at a few specialized housing markets that you might want to consider when adding to your portfolio. By doing so, you'll not only increase your income by hitting a group of renters that you normally wouldn't have access to (such as college students), but you may also get that warm feeling that comes from providing housing to those who face obstacles when getting adequate housing (such as disabled individuals).

Joining the Fray

One of the best parts of catering to specialized housing markets is knowing that tenants will pretty much always be out there, eager to get into your property, and also that the competition for those renters is lower than it would be if you were managing a more traditional property.

In other words, if you own a three-unit home in a college town, the chance of that property being rented out for most of the year to willing individuals (and/or their financially capable parents) is very good. The same goes for the owner of the affordable duplex that's clean and well kept, yet fetches a lower rental rate due to its location in a less desirable part of town.

IMPORTANT NOTE

There will always be demand for nontraditional housing that appeals to specialized markets, but working in this market requires a more focused approach to property management that centers around targeting the right groups of renters, equipping the units properly, and pricing them at a rate that the targeted sector can afford to pay.

Let's look at some of the specialized housing markets that you'll want to consider as you build your property management business.

Workforce Housing

With the residential market experiencing record price gains over the last few years, at least one group of buyers has been finding itself locked out of the American Dream: first-time home buyers who need affordable or workforce housing (defined as for-rent or for-sale housing developed for residents who work in the communities in which the housing is located).

Add in the fact that the subprime mortgage market—often thought of as the best financing source for this group of buyer—experienced a downward spiral of its own, and you get a recipe for disaster.

"We believe that a lack of affordable housing is the number-one reason people become homeless," says the community relations manager for the Homeless Coalition of Hillsborough County, in Tampa, Florida. "Many people aren't making enough money to afford the fair market rents or sale prices here, where there is a deficit between the number of units needed and the number of units currently available."

That sentiment echoed across the country in 2007 and 2008, when mortgages became harder to come by, housing prices remained high, and buyers significantly slowed the activity that they'd built up over the prior years.

The good news is that those seeking affordable housing make great tenant candidates for any property manager whose units are priced at or below market rates and are located in areas where people only commute a short distance to work. Also falling under this category are workers like teachers and law enforcement personnel, who are highly valued but tend to earn low wages for their hard work.

You can carve a niche in the property management field by acquiring property that appeals to these types of tenants and then advertising your unit(s) in places where such individuals tend to frequent. Bulletin boards at the local library might be an age-old strategy, for example, but they can work when trying to reach teachers and other individuals who would make great tenants for your property.

Disabled Access

Disabled individuals face significant challenges when trying to find a place to live, but they also have significant protections that help them get through the obstacles. The first one is the most important: as a property manager, you can't ask the person if he or she has a disability or illness, nor can you ask to see medical records. You will have to provide accommodations, and you will likely have to allow the person to make reasonable modifications to your property (at his or her expense).

IMPORTANT NOTE

Signed into law in 1990, the Americans with Disabilities Act (ADA) makes it unlawful to discriminate against people with disabilities. By the ADA's definition, an individual is considered disabled if he or she has one of the following: (1) a physical or mental impairment that substantially limits one or more major life activities, (2) a record of such impairment, and (3) is regarded as having such an impairment.

As a property manager, you can't discriminate against disabled individuals, but you can create accommodations that makes their lives more comfortable...thus intentionally targeting these renters. The federal Fair Housing Act and Fair Housing Amendments Act (42 U.S. Code §§3601–3619, 3631) prohibit discrimination against people who:

Have a physical or mental disability that substantially limits one or more major life activities—including, but not limited to:

- Mobility impairments
- Hearing impairments
- Visual impairments
- Chronic alcoholism (if it is being addressed through a recovery program)
- Mental illness
- HIV, AIDS, and AIDS-Related Complex or mental retardation
- A history of such a disability or are regarded by others as though they have such a disability

Do Your Homework

Groups like the U.S. Department of Housing and Urban Development (HUD), HOPE for Homeowners, and the Center for Independent Living offer courses and seminars (many times free of charge) on subjects like fair housing laws, financing programs for the disabled, and ADA accessibility laws. These educational sources will give you an inside view of what it's really like to be disabled, the programs available for renters, the challenges they face in the housing market, and the laws that protect them.

IMPORTANT NOTE

Keeping up on ADA laws is important for the property owner who needs to know, for example, whether or not multifamily residences are complying with the laws of accessibility.

As a landlord, you'll need to pay particular attention to the accommodations in your unit, and whether they are adequate for disabled individuals. Someone without disabilities probably wouldn't immediately notice the width of a doorway, for example, but to a person using a wheelchair, that measurement can be critical. The doorways in most homes and multifamily dwellings built in the 1970s and early 1980s are two and a half feet wide—not wide enough for a wheelchair.

By law, new buildings must have 36-inch doorways. Hallways must be also wide enough for someone to travel down the hall and turn into a room. In the bathroom, there must be room to wheel in, turn around, and shut the door.

To effectively reach the disabled market, try advertising your vacancies at VA and rehabilitation hospitals. Many of these facilities will let you attend the meetings held for their patients, thus expanding your chances of reaching out to people who would make great tenants for your properties.

Student Units

Student housing is a popular choice for property managers whose units are located in close proximity to a college or university. Every fall, a slew of new, prospective tenants converges on campus, hoping to live somewhere other than a cramped dorm. Sometimes they live in groups, while others live alone or in pairs. Either way, these renters tend to make good customers for anyone who doesn't mind a complaint call once in a while about a wild party being held at their property.

CompleteLandlord.com offers a variety of webinars that focus on helping landlords achieve maximum success. Learn more online at www.completelandlord.com/store.aspx#kits&software.

Seriously though, student housing presents a significant opportunity for landlords who can fetch premium rates for their properties and have the cost split between two or more families. In such arrangements—typically called *off-campus housing* by the universities themselves—both landlord and tenant have rights and responsibilities.

The University of California, for example, encourages students to read leases thoroughly and understand that based on the state's Civil Code 1941, a landlord is obligated to provide:

◆ Effective protection against the elements (i.e., roof and walls that do not leak).

◆ Plumbing facilities that function properly, including hot and cold running water and sewage disposal.
◆ Working heating facilities.
◆ Properly maintained electrical wiring.
◆ A sanitary building and grounds free from debris, filth, rodents, cockroaches, and so on.
◆ Adequate garbage receptacles.
◆ Floors, stairways, and railings that are in good repair.
◆ Reasonable notice (usually 24 hours) to enter your apartment unless there is an emergency.

At the same time, the tenant must:

◆ Keep the premises clean and undamaged.
◆ Dispose of garbage and trash properly (unless the landlord has agreed to do this).
◆ Use all electrical, gas, and plumbing fixtures properly and keep them as clean as their condition permits.
◆ Keep any person on the premises with permission from willfully damaging the premises or the facilities.
◆ Use each room only for the purpose for which it was intended.
◆ Inform the landlord of all roommate changes.

One of the best ways to reach college-age renters is through college or university bulletin boards (both online and the old-fashioned kind that are tacked up in the library and recreational areas), which are often perused by individuals looking for somewhere off campus to live. Be sure to hit the streets early with your advertising strategy because many students have to lock in their living arrangements for the coming semester months before they actually arrive on campus.

IMPORTANT NOTE

There isn't any certain type of house that is more appealing to a gay or lesbian couple, for example, but this is a market that can be effectively targeted by property managers who would like to occupy units with nontraditional individuals, couples, or families.

Expanding Your Horizons

As a property manager, the world is your oyster when it comes to finding tenants. You can opt for the traditional catch-all approach by casting a wide net for whatever bites, or you can narrow your options and set your sights on a specific group of individuals that you *know* would make good tenants who pay on time and take care of your properties as if they were their own.

In the next chapter, we'll delve further into affordable and Section 8 housing as two more options that you will want to consider as you build your property management empire.

CHAPTER 18

Affordable Housing, Section 8, and Discrimination

We covered some of the fine points of working in the affordable housing market in the last chapter, so now we'll go over the legalities of working in this market. Many of the rules are simply common sense, while a few are detailed and require a more in-depth knowledge in order to follow them properly.

Let's start with the Section 8 program, which is now more commonly known as the Housing Choice Voucher program. It's a housing assistance program funded by the U.S. Department of Housing and Urban Development (HUD), and something you should be familiar with as a property manager.

Tenants qualify for the program if their income is below a certain level. This level, in addition to other criteria, varies according to state. Qualified tenants rent properties that are preapproved and meet requirements for minimal size, condition, and amenities.

The properties can be apartments, duplexes, or single-family homes. The tenant pays part of the rent directly to the landlord, and the government, specifically, a local public housing agency (PHA), pays the remainder of the rent.

The benefit of accepting tenants through the Housing Choice Voucher program is you are guaranteed that at least a portion of the rent will be paid. Even if tenants should break their lease or you evict them, the local PHA will continue to pay their portion of the rent.

If you decide to enroll as a Housing Choice Voucher landlord, contact your local PHA. They will provide the paperwork, inspect your property to make sure it meets necessary requirements and, ultimately, pay you the government's portion directly.

To find your local PHA office, visit HUD's web site (www.hud.gov) and click on the link to your state.

IMPORTANT NOTE

Remember, you should follow the same methods of screening and approving potential Housing Choice Voucher tenants that you would use for others. The PHA will qualify tenants to ensure they can get assistance, but the rest is up to you.

The same rules apply to these tenants as other tenants: you can collect a security deposit (from them, not the government), charge them late fees as stated in your lease, and evict them, if necessary.

What You Need to Know about Section 8

The team at CompleteLandlord.com receives frequent requests for information about subsidized housing and Section 8 tenants. The following is a list of facts about Section 8 guidelines that every landlord should know:

- A Section 8 housing development can reject a qualified applicant.
- Applicants with a history of drug use and drug-related criminal activity can be rejected. Also, landlords are not required to rent to applicants with a poor credit rating. A prospective tenant with no credit history, however, cannot be rejected on this basis.
- An applicant can never be rejected on the basis of race, color, religion, sex, familial status, national origin, disability, or age. A single-parent household or a family receiving welfare benefits cannot be rejected for their status as well.
- In addition to low-income families, there are others who are entitled to receive Section 8 rental vouchers.
- Elderly and disabled individuals can also qualify for vouchers.
- A private landlord does not have to rent to a tenant with a Section 8 voucher.

(continued)

What You Need to Know about Section 8 (*Continued*)

- Only landlords who participate in the program (including companies that own and operate apartment complexes) are required to take tenants with vouchers.
- A landlord can evict a Section 8 tenant.
- A Section 8 tenant can be evicted for good cause. Good cause includes failure to pay rent, criminal activity, or repeated behavior that seriously affects the health and welfare of other tenants.
- Section 8 tenants have certain rights if a landlord attempts to evict them. The tenant can contest the notice of eviction by requesting a hearing with the local housing authority.

Don't Discriminate

All property managers like to think that they're following the rules of the road when it comes to sticky issues like discrimination. Unfortunately, some get caught in the web (sometimes unintentionally) and have to prove that they're complying with ADA and the Fair Housing Act, both of which apply in an industry where discrimination because of race, sex, creed, religion, or disability is unacceptable.

Landlords must accommodate the needs of disabled tenants, within reason, at the landlord's own expense (42 U.S.C. §3604(f)(3)(B)). Disabled tenants may expect their landlords to reasonably adjust rules, procedures, or services in order to provide an equal opportunity to use and enjoy a dwelling unit or a common space. Accommodations can include such things as parking: If the landlord provides parking in the first place, providing a close-in, spacious parking space would be an accommodation for a tenant who uses a wheelchair.

And while landlords are expected to accommodate reasonable requests, they need not undertake changes that would seriously impair their ability to run their business. For example, if an applicant who uses crutches prefers the third-story apartment in a walk-up building to the one on the ground floor, the landlord does not have to rip the building apart to install an elevator. That expense would be unreasonable.

Landlords must also allow disabled tenants to make reasonable modifications to their living unit or common areas at their expense, if needed for the person to comfortably and safely live in the unit. That person has the right to modify the living space to the extent necessary to make the space safe and comfortable, as long as the modifications will not make the unit unacceptable to the next tenant, or if the existing tenants agrees and is financially able to undo the modification when he or she permanently vacates the premises.

What Can Be Modified?

Examples of modifications undertaken by a disabled tenant include:

- Lowering countertops for a tenant who uses a wheelchair
- Installing special faucets or door handles for persons with limited hand use
- Modifying kitchen appliances to accommodate a blind tenant
- Installing a ramp to allow wheelchair access to a raised living room

These modifications must be reasonable and made with prior approval. A landlord is entitled to ask for a description of the proposed modifications, proof that they will be done in a workman-like manner, and evidence that the tenant is obtaining any necessary building permits. In addition, if a tenant proposes to modify the unit in a way that will require restoration when he or she leaves (such as the repositioning of lowered kitchen counters), the landlord may require that tenant to pay into an interest-bearing escrow account the amount estimated for the restoration. (The interest will belong to the tenant.)

Fair Housing Act

The Fair Housing Act prohibits discrimination in the sale, rental, and financing of dwellings and in other housing-related transactions based on race, color, national origin, religion, sex, familial status (including children under the age of 18 living with parents of legal custodians, pregnant women, and people securing custody of children under the age of 18), and disability.

The act covers most types of housing, but exempts (in some cases) owner-occupied buildings with no more than four units, single-family housing sold or rented without the use of a broker, and housing operated by organizations and private clubs that limit occupancy to members.

Actions prohibited by the Fair Housing Act include (but aren't limited to): the refusal to rent or sell housing; the refusal to negotiate for housing; making housing unavailable; denying a dwelling; setting different terms, conditions, or privileges for sale or rental of a dwelling; or falsely denying that housing is available for inspection, sale, or rental.

The Fair Housing Act also prohibits anyone from advertising or making any statement of preference based on race, color, national origin, religion, sex, familial status, or handicap. This prohibition against discriminatory advertising applies to single-family and owner-occupied housing that is otherwise exempt from the Fair Housing Act.

Play by the Rules

In our increasingly litigious society, it's important that property managers follow the rules carefully when selecting, renting to, and evicting tenants. These three junctures tend to present the most obstacles and should be entered into carefully, particularly if you see any possible sign of a problem down the road.

Using a combination of common sense, the information you're learning from this book, and the good advice that you'll find online at CompleteLandlord.com, you'll be able to avoid any tangles with tenants and/or law over possible discriminatory practices.

CHAPTER 19

Continuing Your Property Management Education

In your hands, you hold a book that's based on the tried-and-true CompleteLandlord.com system for managing properties. The information between its covers should be enough to get your landlording business off the ground and running in the right direction. Expect to learn more as you go along on your own, from the CompleteLandlord.com professionals and members, and from other professionals in the industry. You'll also learn from your own mistakes and from the mistakes that others before you have made.

Ongoing Resources

As for your continuing education, there are plenty of books, web sites, and even classes available that cover owning and managing a rental property. Since you have already read this book, you have a good grounding about what your landlording responsibilities and workload will be.

Here are some suggestions to fill in the gaps as you continue your education:

◆ *Stay up-to-date.* To ensure that you keep up with changing laws, rules, and trends regarding rental properties, check out www .completelandlord.com for the latest information and updates on real estate investing. You'll find a wealth of resources at your fingertips and a complete system for landlording success at this site.

◆ *Learn your state laws regarding landlords and tenants.* You can access a list of laws by state at www.landlord.com/legal main.htm. Check this site—or ask your local housing agency—to find out your obligations on security deposits, disclosures, and much more.

◆ *Join a local landlord association.* Learn from the experiences of other landlords—and use them to get references for contractors, real estate agents, and even tenants. An association is an excellent source of information on everything from the current rental market to how to perform a complicated repair. Search for an association near you at www.realestateassociations.com/index.html or www.landlord.com/assoc_main.htm.

◆ *Keep an eye on the classified ads.* Even if you have a tenant who is only two months into his or her yearlong lease, in the interest of keeping your pipeline full, you should be checking the For Rent ads in your local newspaper. It pays to have an idea of how many properties are for rent, the amount of rent that is asked, and how long those properties are advertised. You want to have a big picture of the rental market so that you will know if it will be tough or easy to get another tenant, and how much rent you can charge. The rental market can change constantly, so make this an ongoing research project.

Don't get complacent about legal issues, your local rental market, or trends in landlording (such as new tenant scams)—there will always be something new to surprise you in this field. With the help of CompleteLandlord.com and the resources listed in this book, you will be prepared to face new challenges with your rental property and tenants.

The End

Thus ends the lesson in property management. With your newfound knowledge, your skills, some hard work, and a little luck, you should be able to translate your rental property into the foundation of your financial security. Good luck with your landlording business!

Appendixes

APPENDIX A

Summary of Icon Information

Money Savers

These sections are designed to save you money. Use the information in them to make frugal decisions regarding your cash outlay when investing in and running your properties.

Money Makers

Here's where you'll learn how to make money in real estate. Ferret out the best possible tips and advice from these sections of the book and you'll be well braced to earn a living and more from your real estate investments.

Time Savers

We know there are only so many hours in a day, so use these areas of the book to shave precious time from your schedule and maximize the time spent on your landlording and real estate investment business.

APPENDIX B

Tour of the CompleteLandlord Site with Free Trial Membership Offer

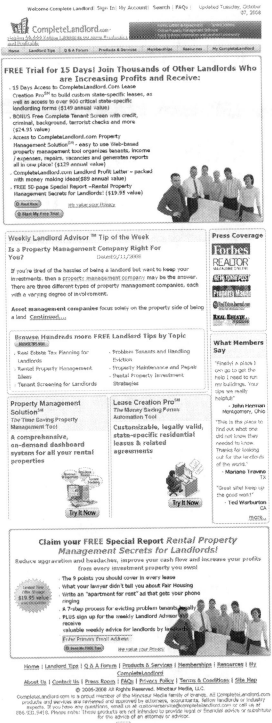

CompleteLandlord.com

Home | Landlord Tips | Q & A Forum | Products & Services | Memberships | Resources | My CompleteLandlord

FREE Trial for 15 Days! Join Thousands of Other Landlords Who are Increasing Profits and Receive:

- 15 Days Access to CompleteLandlord.Com Lease Creation Pro℠ to build custom state-specific leases, as well as access to over 900 critical state-specific landlording forms ($149 annual value)
- BONUS Free Complete Tenant Screen with credit, criminal, background, terrorist checks and more ($24.95 value)
- Access to CompleteLandlord.com Property Management Solution℠ - easy to use Web-based property management tool organizes tenants, income / expenses, repairs, vacancies and generates reports all in one place! ($129 annual value)
- CompleteLandlord.com Landlord Profit Letter – packed with money making ideas($89 annual value)
- FREE 50-page Special Report –Rental Property Management Secrets for Landlords! ($19.95 value)

Read More   We value your Privacy
Start My Free Trial

Weekly Landlord Advisor ™ Tip of the Week

Is a Property Management Company Right For You?
Dated2/11/2008

If you're tired of the hassles of being a landlord but want to keep your investments, then a property management company may be the answer. There are three different types of property management companies, each with a varying degree of involvement.

Asset management companies focus solely on the property side of being a land Continued....

Browse Hundreds more FREE Landlord Tips by Topic

- Real Estate Tax Planning for Landlords
- Rental Property Management Ideas
- Tenant Screening for Landlords
- Problem Tenants and Handling Eviction
- Property Maintenance and Repair
- Rental Property Investment Strategies

Property Management Solution℠
The Time Saving Property Management Tool

A comprehensive, on-demand dashboard system for all your rental properties

Try It Now

Lease Creation Pro℠
The Money Saving Forms Automation Tool

Customizable, legally valid, state-specific residential leases & related agreements

Try It Now

Press Coverage

Forbes
REALTOR
NEW YORK POST

What Members Say

"Finally! A place I can go to get the help I need to run my buildings. Your tips are really helpful!"
- John Herman Montgomery, Ohio

"This is the place to find out what one did not know they needed to know. Thanks for looking out for the landlords of the world."
- Mariano Travino TX

"Great site! Keep up the good work!"
- Ted Warburton CA

more...

Claim your FREE Special Report *Rental Property Management Secrets for Landlords!*

Reduce aggravation and headaches, improve your cash flow and increase your profits from every investment property you own!

- The 9 points you should cover in every lease
- What your lawyer didn't tell you about Fair Housing
- Write an "apartment for rent" ad that gets your phone ringing
- A 7-step process for evicting problem tenants legally
- PLUS sign up for the weekly Landlord Advisor and receive valuable weekly advice for landlords by landlords

Enter Primary Email Address

Send Me FREE Tips   We value your Privacy

CompleteLandlord.com

Helping 53,000 Fellow Landlords be More Productive and Profitable

+ Forms, Letters & Agreements
+ Online Property Management Software
+ Need-to-Know Information and Landlord Community
+ Tenant Screens

| Home | Landlord Tips | Q & A Forum | Products & Services | Memberships | Resources | My CompleteLandlord |

CompleteLandlord.com Forum

Please click on a Category below to begin or view a Topic.

Categories	Topics covered in this Category	Topics
Buying property	Acquiring rental properties	23
Cash Flow	Maximizing your income	12
completelandlord.com	Completelandlord.com product line	10
Contractors	Vendors, contractors and other workers	8
Disclosures	Lead paint, asbestos and more	4
Discrimination	Rentals and fair housing	8
Eviction	Dealing with problem tenants	72
Insurance	Protecting your assets	3
Landscaping	Lawn and garden	10
Late Fees	Rent collection and fees	13
Leases	Signing the agreements and customized forms	45
Legal	Understanding the law	31
Maintenance & Repairs	Fixing issues and preventive work	27
Managing 1031 Exchanges	"Starker" transactions and trading up	2
Marketing	Getting the word out	2
Miscellaneous	Questions that don't fit into any category listed	46
New Landlords	Just starting	14
Non Payment	When things go south	13
Notices to Tenants	Communicating with residents	2
Pets	Dealing with animals	8
Property Management	The big picture	19
Rent collection	Getting residents to pay	7
Section 8	Public assistance programs	5
Security	Maintaining a safe place to live	3
Security Deposits	Handling the deposit	31
Selling Property	Disposing of rental properties	9
Software / Books	Resources	2
Students	Renting to college students	2
Taxes	Landlords and the government	15
Tenant Screening	Checking credit, employment, etc.	16
Tenants	Our customer	13
Utilities	Keeping the lights, electric, gas and cable on	7

Need Help?
Or first time?
CLICK HERE

Top Ten Topics

1. Withholding a Security/Damage Deposit (11 replies)

2. Failure to return a signed lease (10 replies)

3. What to do with my tenant (9 replies)

4. Management Company Fees (8 replies)

5. How much is enough? (8 replies)

6. Are Tenant Screenings Worth the Cost? (8 replies)

7. tenant breaking lease (7 replies)

8. DO I need to use a lawyer? (6 replies)

9. Newbie Question (6 replies)

10. When to pay a contractor (5 replies)

Add to Favorites

Home | Landlord Tips | Q & A Forum | Products & Services | Memberships | Resources | My CompleteLandlord
About Us | Contact Us | Press Room | FAQs | Privacy Policy | Terms & Conditions | Site Map

© 2006-2008 All Rights Reserved. Minotaur Media, LLC.

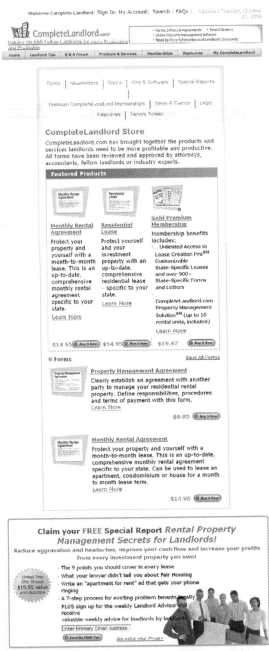

CompleteLandlord.com

Helping 50,000 Fellow Landlords to be More Productive and Profitable

Save Time. Save Money. Make Money. $$$

Home | Landlord Tips | Q & A Forum | Products & Services | Memberships | Resources | My CompleteLandlord

Browse weekly Landlord Advisor Tips

View All

Choose a Topic Below, and Read all the Tips in that Topic.

Real Estate Tax Planning for Landlords

The bad news about being a landlord is that all of the income that you earn from your rental units is subject to federal and state income taxes.

The good news is that tax planning for your rental property opens up many opportunities for sizable tax deductions. Although you may not actually file the taxes on your rental property yourself, as a landlord, it is very important to be familiar with tax deductions so you can keep the appropriate paper documentation for your tax records.

CompleteLandlord.com can help you with your tax planning to save you thousands of dollars and needless headaches with useful advice.

Rental Property Management ideas

Whether you run your rental property business yourself or have a management team working with you, managing rental property has many legal facets every landlord should be knowledgeable about.

CompleteLandlord.com has put together the most important tips that will help you with your rental property management.

This section includes many topics of interest including official leases, tenant policies and special deposits. Remember, doing some of these activities yourself can end up decreasing your management costs.

Top Ten Tips

<Prev   1 2 3 4 5 6 7 8 9 10 ...   Next>

02/11/2008 **Is a Property Management Company Right For You?**
Topic: Property Management

02/04/2008 **Increase Your Bottom Line with Coin-Operated Laundry Machines**

<Prev   1 2 3 4 5 6 7 8 9 10 .   Next>

Submit Your Tip and Earn $25

Submit a tip that gets published by CompleteLandlord.com and you will receive $25.

To learn more Click Here

174

CompleteLandlord.com~

Dashboard | **Properties** | Tenants | Accounting | Tasks | Documents | Reports

Admin

| Properties || Units || Listings || Important Numbers || Announcements || Help |

Properties [Add Property]

Search Criteria

Property State

ALL
Illinois
Idaho

Status

Active

Sort by

Name

Ascending

[Search]

Legend

Hover over the images for more information.

Resident statements on

Resident statements off

Update property images

Property set up for electronic payments

Export data

Property	City	Status	Type		
Devonshire Bldg 1	Darien	Active	Rental		
Jay's Apartments	Chicago	Active	Rental		
K&C Apartments	Independence	Active	Rental		
sample	albama	Active	Rental		
Sample Property	Chicago	Active	Rental		
Socrates House 10	Chicago	Active	Rental		
staci	independence	Active	Rental		
Test property	Chicago	Active	Rental		
test123	chicago	Active	Rental		

Showing 1 - 9 of 9

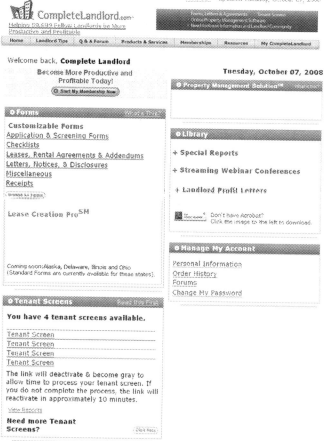

CompleteLandlord.com

Helping 59,599 Fellow Landlords be More
Productive and Profitable

Forms, Letters & Agreements   Tenant Screens
Online Property Management Software
Need-to-Know Information and Landlord Community

Home | Landlord Tips | Q & A Forum | Products & Services | Memberships | Resources | My CompleteLandlord

Welcome back, **Complete Landlord**

Become More Productive and
Profitable Today!

○ Start My Membership Now

Tuesday, October 07, 2008

○ Property Management Solution℠ What's This?

○ Forms What's This?

Customizable Forms
Application & Screening Forms
Checklists
Leases, Rental Agreements & Addendums
Letters, Notices, & Disclosures
Miscellaneous
Receipts

Browse All Forms

Lease Creation Pro℠

○ Library

+ **Special Reports**

+ **Streaming Webinar Conferences**

+ **Landlord Profit Letters**

Don't have Acrobat?
Click the image to the left to download.

Coming soon: Alaska, Delaware, Illinois and Ohio
(Standard Forms are currently available for these states).

○ Manage My Account

Personal Information
Order History
Forums
Change My Password

○ Tenant Screens Read this First

You have 4 tenant screens available.

Tenant Screen
Tenant Screen
Tenant Screen
Tenant Screen

The link will deactivate & become gray to
allow time to process your tenant screen. If
you do not complete the process, the link will
reactivate in approximately 10 minutes.

View Reports

**Need more Tenant
Screens?** Click Here

Add A New Report

Applicant Details   Employment   Landlord

	Last Name	First Name	MI	Gen	SS·#	Birth Date	Age	Driver's License
Applicant:				▼				

	Hse-#	Dir	Street Name	Type	Apt-#	City	State	Zip	County	
Current:		▼		▼			▼			+LL
Previous:		▼		▼			▼			+LL

Credit   Eviction   Criminal

	Experian
Applicant:	☑
Report Type:	CREDIT PROFILE ▼
Credit Grantor Address:	☐
Fraud Detection:	☐
Risk Score:	FICO II (BASE MODEL) ▼
Permissible Purpose:	R/E-REAL ESTATE SPEC ▼

Initial Service Request: _____

End User Reference: _____

[Submit]   <u>HELP</u>

	ORDER	
Applicant		Other
XPN		
EVC		
CRM NT		

Welcome

Welcome to the **CompleteLandlord.com Lease Creation Pro for Alabama**, which enables you to generate a lease and other related documents for you and your tenant.

What kind of agreement do you want to create?

- ○ Residential Lease (fixed-term, such as one year)
- ○ Monthly Rental Agreement (month-to-month)
- ○ Lease with Purchase Option (fixed-term with option to purchase)

Every lease package contains a variety of bonus forms that are optional for your use:

-- Rental & Credit Application
-- Pre-Lease & Post-Lease Inspections
-- Security Deposit Receipt
-- Receipt for Payment of Rent
-- Lead Paint Disclosure form & pamphlet (if required)
-- Garage & Parking Space Agreement
-- Pet Agreement Addendum & Pet Policy

Next   Progress:8 %

5.4.2.1077

179

Welcome

Welcome to the **CompleteLandlord.com Lease Creation Pro for Alabama**, which enables you to generate a lease and other related documents for you and your tenant.

What kind of agreement do you want to create?

○ Residential Lease (fixed-term, such as one year)
○ Monthly Rental Agreement (month-to-month)
○ Lease with Purchase Option (fixed-term with option to purchase)

Every lease package contains a variety of bonus forms that are optional for your use:

-- Rental & Credit Application
-- Pre-Lease & Post-Lease Inspections
-- Security Deposit Receipt
-- Receipt for Payment of Rent
-- Lead Paint Disclosure form & pamphlet (if required)
-- Garage & Parking Space Agreement
-- Pet Agreement Addendum & Pet Policy

Next   Progress: 8 %

5.4.2.1077

☞ Alabama Lease Creation Pro   ⊕ History

Residential Lease- Page 1 of 6

Complete a Residential Lease for Alabama.

What is the date of this lease agreement?
10/6/2008
Hint: This is the date on which you are drafting the lease agreement, i.e. today's date.

What is the name of the landlord(s)?
Hint: Click on the "Add Row" button if there is more than one landlord.

[ ]   Remove

     Add Row

What is the name of the tenant(s)?
Hint: Click on the "Add Row" button if more than one tenant is on the lease.

[ ]   Remove

     Add Row

What is the street address of the rental unit?
(e.g. 123 Main Street)

(e.g. Clark Suites, Apt 1 G)

In what city?

In what county?

In what zip code?

Describe the rental unit.

(e.g. Front 3-bedroom unit on second floor of red brick 4-flat)

Is the rental unit furnished?
◇ Yes ◇ No
Hint: If the apartment is furnished, please attach a list of furnishings and appliances as an addendum to this lease.

On what date does the lease start?
10/6/2008

How long is the lease term (in months)?
12   month(s)
(e.g. 12)

☞ Back ☞ Next ▮ | Progress 17 % |

5.4.2.1077

CompleteLandlord.com™

CompleteLandlord.com Lease Creation Pro™

MY LEASES   Past 30 Dr

STREET ADDRESS	TENANT	STATE	LEASE TYPE	DATE CREATED	EDIT	DELETE
123 Main Steet Clark Suites, Apt 1 G	Samantha Gates	Alabama	Residential Lease	10/6/2008	✎	🗑

 Alabama Garage & Parking Space Agreement for Tenant Samantha Gates.rtf
   Distributed : 10/6/2008 3:58:03 PM

 Alabama Receipt for Payment of Rent for Tenant Samantha Gates.rtf
   Distributed : 10/6/2008 4:05:30 PM

 Alabama Residential Lease for Tenant Samantha Gates.rtf
   Distributed : 10/6/2008 3:52:15 PM

 Alabama Security Deposit Receipt for Tenant Samantha Gates.rtf
   Distributed : 10/6/2008 4:05:30 PM

Create a New Lease

Select a state ▾ (Start)

Coming soon:Alaska, Delaware, Illinois and Ohio,
(Standard Forms are currently available for these states)

CompleteLandlord.com™

Dashboard | Properties | Tenants | Accounting | Tasks | Documents | Reports | Admin

| Dashboard | | My Info | | Preferences | | Support |

My Dashboard

Applications waiting to be accepted or rejected

Submitted	Ref #	Name	Property	Unit
11/08/07 02:46:46 PM EST	1486APP1292	sam lech123244	HYD	2

Tip

The dashboard serves as your command center, highlighting things that require your attention.

Leases ending within 90 days
You have no leases that are ending in the next 90 days.

Vacant Rental Units

Property	Unit	Since
Devonshire Bldg 1	B	
Devonshire Bldg 1	C	
Devonshire Bldg 1	D	
Jay's Apartments	101	
Jay's Apartments	102	
K&C Apartments	1001	
K&C Apartments	1003	
K&C Apartments	1004	
K&C Apartments	1005	
Sample Property	101	
Sample Property	102	
Sample Property	103	
Sample Property	104	
Sample Property	200	
Test property	401	
Test property	501	
Test property	601	
test123	1	
test123	2	
test123	3	
test123	4	
test123	5	

Tasks not yet assigned
You have no unassigned tasks.

My open tasks
You have no new or open tasks.

CompleteLandlord.com™

| Dashboard | Properties | Tenants | Accounting | Tasks | Documents | Reports |
| Admin |

| Properties | | Units | | Listings | | Important Numbers | | Announcements | | Help |

Properties [Add Property]

Search Criteria

Property State:

| ALL |
| Illinois |
| Idaho |

Status:

Active

Sort by:

Name

Ascending

[Search]

Export data

Property	City	Status	Type		
Devonshire Bldg 1	Darien	Active	Rental		
Jay's Apartments	Chicago	Active	Rental		
K&C Apartments	Independence	Active	Rental		
Sample Property	Chicago	Active	Rental		
Socrates House 10	Chicago	Active	Rental		
staci	Independence	Active	Rental		
Test property	Chicago	Active	Rental		
test123	chicago	Active	Rental		

Showing 1 - 8 of 8

Legend

Hover over the images for more information.

- Resident statements on
- Resident statements off
- Update property images
- Property set up for electronic payments

CompleteLandlord.com

Dashboard | Properties | Tenants | Accounting | Tasks | Documents | Reports
Admin

| Properties | Units || Listings || Important Numbers || Announcements || Help |

Search Criteria

Property State:

| ALL |
| Illinois |
| Idaho |

Status:

Active

Sort by

Name

Ascending

[Search]

Legend

Hover over the images for more information.

Resident statements on

Resident statements off

Update property images

Property set up for electronic payments

Properties [Add Property]

Export data

Property	City	Status	Type		
Devonshire Bldg 1	Darien	Active	Rental		
Jay's Apartments	Chicago	Active	Rental		
K&C Apartments					
Sample Property					
Socrates House 10					
staci					
Test property					
test123					

Showing 1 – 8 of 8

Add Property Wizard

* Required

Property Info

Property Name *	
Address *	
City *	
State/Province *	
Zip *	
Type *	Rental
Operating Account *	
Number of Units ⊕ *	1

[Next]

185

CompleteLandlord.com™

| Dashboard | Properties | Tenants | Accounting | Tasks | Documents | Reports |

Admin

| Properties || Units || Listings || Important Numbers || Announcements || Help |

Units [Add Unit]

Search Criteria

Property:

| ALL |
| Devonshire |
| Jay's Apart |

Bedrooms:

| ALL |
| Studio |
| 1 Bed |

Unit (contains):

Sort by:

Property

Ascending

[Search]

Legend

Hover over the images for more information.

⌂ Update Listing Information

Export data

Property - Unit	Name(s)	Bed	Bath	
Devonshire Bldg 1 - D		1 Bed	1 Bath	⌂
Devonshire Bldg 1 - B		2 Bed	1.5 Bath	⌂
Devonshire Bldg 1 - C		2 Bed	1.5 Bath	⌂
Devonshire Bldg 1 - A	Tammy Tenant	3 Bed	1.5 Bath	⌂
Jay's Apartments - 100	Andrea Austrums			⌂
Jay's Apartments - 101				⌂
Jay's Apartments - 102				⌂
K&C Apartments - 1001				⌂
K&C Apartments - 1002	Bob Smith			⌂
K&C Apartments - 1003				⌂
K&C Apartments - 1004				⌂
K&C Apartments - 1005				⌂
sample - 1				⌂
Sample Property - 101				⌂
Sample Property - 102				⌂
Sample Property - 103				⌂
Sample Property - 104				⌂
Sample Property - 200		1 Bed	1.5 Bath	⌂
Test property - 401				⌂
Test property - 501				⌂
Test property - 601				⌂
test123 - 1				⌂
test123 - 2				⌂
test123 - 3				⌂
test123 - 4				⌂
test123 - 5				⌂

Showing 1 - 28 of 28

CompleteLandlord.com~

Dashboard | Properties | Tenants | Accounting | Tasks | Documents | Reports | Admin

| Tenants | | Leases | | Rental Applications | | Outstanding Balances | | Mailings | | Help |

Search Criteria

Status:
All Current

Access Rights:
Active

Property Name:
ALL

Name (contains):

Unit (contains):

Sort by:
Name
Ascending

[Search]

Tenants [Move In | Receive Payment | Enter Meter Readings | Enter Bulk Charges]

Export data

	Name	Phone	Property	Unit		
☐	Austrums, Andrea	⚫	Jay's Apartments	100	🖼	🔑
☐	fdd, fdfd	⚫ Ⓗ	staci	1	🖼	🔑
☐	Levendusky, Jenny	⚫	Test property	301	🖼	🔑
☐	Smith, Bob	⚫ Ⓗ Ⓦ	K&C Apartments	1002	🖼	🔑
☐	Tenant, Tammy ↪	⚫ Ⓗ Ⓦ Ⓜ	Devonshire Bldg 1	A	🖼	🔑

Showing 1 - 5 of 5

[Distribute] [Send Welcome Email]

Legend

Hover over the images for more information.

🖼 View ledger

✉ Welcome email sent successfully

✉ Welcome email not sent successfully

☼ Last login

🔑 Login to tenant's site

CompleteLandlord.com™

Dashboard | Properties | **Tenants** | Accounting | Tasks | Documents | Reports | Admin

| Tenants | | **Leases** | | Rental Applications | | Outstanding Balances | | Mailings | | Help |

Search Criteria

Property Name:

All
Devonshire B
Jay's Apartme
K&C Apartme

Lease Status:
All Current

Sort by:
Property
Ascending

Search

Leases [Move In | Receive Payment | Enter Meter Readings | Enter Bulk Charges]

Export data

Property	Unit	Type	Rent	Start	End	
Devonshire Bldg 1	A	Fixed Term	$1,500.00	03/06/08	03/31/09	
Jay's Apartments	100	Fixed Term	$700.00	02/14/08	02/28/09	
K&C Apartments	1002	Fixed Term	$500.00	02/14/08	02/28/09	
staci	1	Fixed Term	$425.00	02/14/08	02/28/09	
Test property	301	Fixed Term	$1,200.00	02/14/08	02/28/09	

Showing 1 - 5 of 5

Legend
Hover over the images
for more information
View lease ledger
Download lease
document
Move out tenant(s)

Lease Ledger [Enter Charge | Receive Payment | Issue Credit | Issue Refund | Apply Deposit to Balances | Print Statement]

Property and Unit #: Devonshire Bldg 1 - A
Tenant(s): Tammy Tenant
Lease Term: 03/06/2008 - 03/31/2009

Payment is due by the 1st of the month
A one time late fee of $5.00 will be charged on the 8th of the month if payment is not received. A daily late fee of $2.00 will be charged on and after the 7th of the month if payment is not received.

Ledger | Ledger By Account | Deposits Held   Last 3 months | Last 12 months | All

	Date	Type	Memo	Account	Increase	Decrease	Balance
	07/07/2008		Balance Forward				$7,500.00
☐	08/01/2008	Charge	Rent	Rent Income	$1,500.00		$9,000.00
☐	09/01/2008	Charge	Rent	Rent Income	$1,500.00		$10,500.00
☐	10/01/2008	Charge	Rent	Rent Income	$1,500.00		$12,000.00

Delete Entries

Recurring Charges [Add Recurring Charge]

Next Charge	Memo	Account	Frequency	Duration	Amount
11/01/2008	Rent	Rent Income	Monthly	Until end of term	1,500.00

188

APPENDIX C

Essential CompleteLandlord Worksheets, Checklists, and Other Forms

Current Customizable Forms and Letters and Recently Revised Available for CompleteLandlord Members at CompleteLandlord.com:

Agreement to Amend Lease Agreement: Washington

Agreement to Amend Lease: Alabama

Agreement to Amend Lease: Arizona

Agreement to Amend Lease: Arkansas

Agreement to Amend Lease: Colorado

Agreement to Amend Lease: Kentucky

Agreement to Amend Lease: Louisiana

Agreement to Amend Lease: Maine

Agreement to Amend Lease: Maryland

Agreement to Amend Lease: Minnesota

Agreement to Amend Lease: Mississippi

Agreement to Amend Lease: Oklahoma

Agreement to Amend Lease: Oregon

Agreement to Amend Lease: South Carolina

Agreement to Amend Lease: Wisconsin

Apartment Lease: New York City

Changing the Locks Notice

Co-Signer Agreement

Collateral Assignment of Lease

Commercial Lease

Commercial Lease: Washington

Commercial Lease: West Virginia

Commercial Lease: Wisconsin

Commercial Lease: Wyoming

Commercial Lease: Alabama

Commercial Lease: Alaska

Commercial Lease: Arizona

Commercial Lease: Arkansas

Commercial Lease: California

Commercial Lease: Colorado

Commercial Lease: Connecticut

Commercial Lease: Delaware

Commercial Lease: Florida

Commercial Lease: Georgia

Commercial Lease: Hawaii

Commercial Lease: Idaho

Disclosure of Information on Lead-Based Paint and/or Lead-Based Paint Hazards: Georgia

Disclosure of Information on Lead-Based Paint and/or Lead-Based Paint Hazards: Hawaii

Disclosure of Information on Lead-Based Paint and/or Lead-Based Paint Hazards: Idaho

Disclosure of Information on Lead-Based Paint and/or Lead-Based Paint Hazards: Illinois

Disclosure of Information on Lead-Based Paint and/or Lead-Based Paint Hazards: Indiana

Disclosure of Information on Lead-Based Paint and/or Lead-Based Paint Hazards: Iowa

Disclosure of Information on Lead-Based Paint and/or Lead-Based Paint Hazards: Kansas

Disclosure of Information on Lead-Based Paint and/or Lead-Based Paint Hazards: Kentucky

Disclosure of Information on Lead-Based Paint and/or Lead-Based Paint Hazards: Louisiana

Disclosure of Information on Lead-Based Paint and/or Lead-Based Paint Hazards: Maine

Disclosure of Information on Lead-Based Paint and/or Lead-Based Paint Hazards: Maryland

Disclosure of Information on Lead-Based Paint and/or Lead-Based Paint Hazards: Massachusetts

Disclosure of Information on Lead-Based Paint and/or Lead-Based Paint Hazards: Michigan

Disclosure of Information on Lead-Based Paint and/or Lead-Based Paint Hazards: Minnesota

Disclosure of Information on Lead-Based Paint and/or Lead-Based Paint Hazards: Mississippi

Disclosure of Information on Lead-Based Paint and/or Lead-Based Paint Hazards: Missouri

Disclosure of Information on Lead-Based Paint and/or Lead-Based Paint Hazards: Montana

Disclosure of Information on Lead-Based Paint and/or Lead-Based Paint Hazards: Nebraska

Disclosure of Information on Lead-Based Paint and/or Lead-Based Paint Hazards: Nevada

Disclosure of Information on Lead-Based Paint and/or Lead-Based Paint Hazards: New Hampshire

Disclosure of Information on Lead-Based Paint and/or Lead-Based Paint Hazards: New Jersey

Disclosure of Information on Lead-Based Paint and/or Lead-Based Paint Hazards: New Mexico

Disclosure of Information on Lead-Based Paint and/or Lead-Based Paint Hazards: New York

Disclosure of Information on Lead-Based Paint and/or Lead-Based Paint Hazards: North Carolina

Disclosure of Information on Lead-Based Paint and/or Lead-Based Paint Hazards: North Dakota

Disclosure of Information on Lead-Based Paint and/or Lead-Based Paint Hazards: Ohio

Garage/Parking Space Lease Agreement: California

Garage/Parking Space Lease Agreement: Colorado

Garage/Parking Space Lease Agreement: Connecticut

Garage/Parking Space Lease Agreement: Delaware

Garage/Parking Space Lease Agreement: District of Columbia

Garage/Parking Space Lease Agreement: Florida

Garage/Parking Space Lease Agreement: Georgia

Garage/Parking Space Lease Agreement: Hawaii

Garage/Parking Space Lease Agreement: Idaho

Garage/Parking Space Lease Agreement: Illinois

Garage/Parking Space Lease Agreement: Indiana

Garage/Parking Space Lease Agreement: Iowa

Garage/Parking Space Lease Agreement: Kansas

Garage/Parking Space Lease Agreement: Kentucky

Garage/Parking Space Lease Agreement: Louisiana

Garage/Parking Space Lease Agreement: Maine

Garage/Parking Space Lease Agreement: Maryland

Garage/Parking Space Lease Agreement: Massachusetts

Garage/Parking Space Lease Agreement: Michigan

Garage/Parking Space Lease Agreement: Minnesota

Garage/Parking Space Lease Agreement: Mississippi

Garage/Parking Space Lease Agreement: Missouri

Garage/Parking Space Lease Agreement: Montana

Garage/Parking Space Lease Agreement: Nebraska

Garage/Parking Space Lease Agreement: Nevada

Garage/Parking Space Lease Agreement: New Hampshire

Garage/Parking Space Lease Agreement: New Jersey

Garage/Parking Space Lease Agreement: New Mexico

Garage/Parking Space Lease Agreement: New York

Garage/Parking Space Lease Agreement: North Carolina

Garage/Parking Space Lease Agreement: North Dakota

Garage/Parking Space Lease Agreement: Ohio

Garage/Parking Space Lease Agreement: Oklahoma

Garage/Parking Space Lease Agreement: Oregon

Garage/Parking Space Lease Agreement: Pennsylvania

Garage/Parking Space Lease Agreement: Rhode Island

Garage/Parking Space Lease Agreement: South Carolina

Garage/Parking Space Lease Agreement: South Dakota

Notice to Pay Rent or Quit for Residential Lease: Massachusetts

Notice to Pay Rent or Quit for Residential Lease: Minnesota

Notice to Pay Rent or Quit for Residential Lease: Wisconsin

Notice to Pay Rent or Quit for Unpaid Check: Virginia

Notice to Pay Rent or Quit-MA

Notice to Pay Rent or Quit-OH

Notice to Pay Rent or Quit-Spanish

Notice to Pay Rent or Quit: Alaska

Notice to Pay Rent or Quit: Arizona

Notice to Pay Rent or Quit: California

Notice to Pay Rent or Quit: Colorado

Notice to Pay Rent or Quit: Delaware

Notice to Pay Rent or Quit: District of Columbia

Notice to Pay Rent or Quit: Florida

Notice to Pay Rent or Quit: Hawaii

Notice to Pay Rent or Quit: Idaho

Notice to Pay Rent or Quit: Illinois

Notice to Pay Rent or Quit: Indiana

Notice to Pay Rent or Quit: Iowa

Notice to Pay Rent or Quit: Kansas

Notice to Pay Rent or Quit: Kentucky

Notice to Pay Rent or Quit: Michigan

Notice to Pay Rent or Quit: Mississippi

Notice to Pay Rent or Quit: Missouri

Notice to Pay Rent or Quit: Montana

Notice to Pay Rent or Quit: Nebraska

Notice to Pay Rent or Quit: Nevada

Notice to Pay Rent or Quit: New Hampshire

Notice to Pay Rent or Quit: New York

Notice to Pay Rent or Quit: North Dakota

Notice to Pay Rent or Quit: Oklahoma

Notice to Pay Rent or Quit: South Dakota

Notice to Pay Rent or Quit: Tennessee

Notice to Pay Rent or Quit: Texas

Notice to Pay Rent or Quit: Utah

Notice to Pay Rent or Quit: Vermont

Notice to Pay Rent or Quit: Virginia

Notice to Pay Rent or Quit: Washington

Notice to Pay Rent or Quit: West Virginia

Notice to Pay Rent or Quit: Wyoming

Notice to Pay Rent Upon Abandonment: West Virginia

Notice to Quit for Breach for Monthly Rental Agreement: Pennsylvania

Notice to Quit for Breach for Monthly Rental Agreement: Wisconsin

Notice to Quit for Breach for Residential Lease: Pennsylvania

Notice to Quit for Breach: Alabama

Notice to Quit for Breach: Hawaii

Notice to Quit for Breach: Illinois

Notice to Quit for Breach: Minnesota

Notice to Quit for Failure to Pay for Utility Service: Alaska

Notice to Quit for Inflicting Substantial Damages to Premises: Alaska

Notice to Quit for Nonpayment of Rent: Arkansas

Notice to Quit for Nonpayment of Rent: Georgia

Notice to Terminate for Recurrence of Noncompliance: Kentucky

Notice to Terminate for Recurrence of Noncompliance: Mississippi

Notice to Terminate for Recurrence of Noncompliance: Montana

Notice to Terminate for Recurrence of Noncompliance: Nebraska

Notice to Terminate for Recurrence of Noncompliance: Oklahoma

Notice to Terminate for Recurrence of Noncompliance: Rhode Island

Notice to Terminate for Recurrence of Noncompliance: Tennessee

Notice to Terminate for Recurrence of Noncompliance: Virginia

Notice to Terminate for Recurrence of Violation of Pet Agreement: Oregon

Notice to Terminate for Recurring Use of Illegal Drugs and Alcohol: Oregon

Notice to Terminate for Use of Illegal Drugs and Alcohol: Oregon

Notice to Terminate for Violation of Pet Agreement: Oregon

Notice to Terminate Monthly Rental Agreement for Conversion or Change: Washington

Notice to Terminate Monthly Rental Agreement for Demolition, Conversion or Change: Hawaii

Notice to Terminate Monthly Rental Agreement in New York City: New York

Notice to Terminate Monthly Rental Agreement Outside New York City: New York

Notice to Terminate Monthly Rental Agreement: Alabama

Notice to Terminate Monthly Rental Agreement: Alaska

Notice to Terminate Monthly Rental Agreement: Arizona

Notice to Terminate Monthly Rental Agreement: Arkansas

Notice to Terminate Monthly Rental Agreement: California

Notice to Terminate Monthly Rental Agreement: Colorado

Notice to Terminate Monthly Rental Agreement: Connecticut

Notice to Terminate Monthly Rental Agreement: Delaware

Notice to Terminate Monthly Rental Agreement: District of Columbia

Notice to Terminate Monthly Rental Agreement: Florida

Notice to Terminate Monthly Rental Agreement: Georgia

Notice to Terminate Monthly Rental Agreement: Hawaii

Notice to Terminate Monthly Rental Agreement: Idaho

Notice to Terminate Monthly Rental Agreement: Illinois

Notice to Terminate Monthly Rental Agreement: Indiana

Notice to Terminate Monthly Rental Agreement: Iowa

Notice to Terminate Monthly Rental Agreement: Kansas

Notice to Terminate Monthly Rental Agreement: Kentucky

Notice to Terminate Monthly Rental Agreement: Louisiana

Notice to Terminate Monthly Rental Agreement: Maryland

Notice to Vacate for Residential Lease: Louisiana

Notice to Vacate: Louisiana

144-Hour Notice to Pay Rent or Quit: Oregon

Past Due Rent Notice

Past-Due Rent: First Notice

Pet Agreement Addendum: Alabama

Pet Agreement Addendum: Alaska

Pet Agreement Addendum: Arizona

Pet Agreement Addendum: Arkansas

Pet Agreement Addendum: California

Pet Agreement Addendum: Colorado

Pet Agreement Addendum: Connecticut

Pet Agreement Addendum: Delaware

Pet Agreement Addendum: District of Columbia

Pet Agreement Addendum: Florida

Pet Agreement Addendum: Georgia

Pet Agreement Addendum: Hawaii

Pet Agreement Addendum: Idaho

Pet Agreement Addendum: Illinois

Pet Agreement Addendum: Indiana

Pet Agreement Addendum: Iowa

Pet Agreement Addendum: Kansas

Pet Agreement Addendum: Kentucky

Pet Agreement Addendum: Louisiana

Pet Agreement Addendum: Maine

Pet Agreement Addendum: Maryland

Pet Agreement Addendum: Massachusetts

Pet Agreement Addendum: Michigan

Pet Agreement Addendum: Minnesota

Pet Agreement Addendum: Mississippi

Pet Agreement Addendum: Missouri

Pet Agreement Addendum: Montana

Pet Agreement Addendum: Nebraska

Pet Agreement Addendum: Nevada

Pet Agreement Addendum: New Hampshire

Pet Agreement Addendum: New Jersey

Pet Agreement Addendum: New Mexico

Pet Agreement Addendum: New York

Pet Agreement Addendum: North Carolina

Pet Agreement Addendum: North Dakota

Pet Agreement Addendum: Ohio

Pet Agreement Addendum: Oklahoma

Pet Agreement Addendum: Oregon

Pet Agreement Addendum: Pennsylvania

Pet Agreement Addendum: Rhode Island

Pet Agreement Addendum: South Carolina

Pet Agreement Addendum: South Dakota

Pet Agreement Addendum: Tennessee

Pet Agreement Addendum: Texas

Pet Agreement Addendum: Utah

Pet Agreement Addendum: Vermont

Pet Agreement Addendum: Virginia

Pet Agreement Addendum: Washington

Pet Agreement Addendum: West Virginia

Pet Agreement Addendum: Wisconsin

Pet Agreement Addendum: Wyoming

Pet Damage to Residence Letter

Pet Damage: First Notice

Receipt for Payment of Rent: Washington

Receipt for Payment of Rent: West Virginia

Receipt for Payment of Rent: Wisconsin

Receipt for Payment of Rent: Wyoming

Receipt of Payment of Rent: Tennessee

Rejection Letter: Bad Credit

Rejection Letter: General

Rejection Letter: References

Release of Breach of Lease by Tenant

Rent Statement

Rental Acceptance Letter

Rental Information Memo

Rental/Credit Application

Rental/Credit Application-Spanish

Renter's Insurance Referral

Request for Rental History Verification

Residential Inventory List

Residential Lease Addendum-Pets

Residential Lease-Furnished

Residential Lease-Spanish

Residential Lease: Alabama

Residential Lease: Alaska

Residential Lease: Arizona

Residential Lease: Arkansas

Residential Lease: California

Residential Lease: Chicago

Residential Lease: Colorado

Residential Lease: Connecticut

Residential Lease: Delaware

Residential Lease: Florida

Residential Lease: Georgia

Residential Lease: Hawaii

Residential Lease: Idaho

Residential Lease: Illinois

Residential Lease: Indiana

Residential Lease: Iowa

Residential Lease: Kansas

Residential Lease: Kentucky

Residential Lease: Louisiana

Residential Lease: Maine

Residential Lease: Maryland

Residential Lease: Massachusetts

Residential Lease: Michigan

Residential Lease: Minnesota

Residential Lease: Mississippi

Residential Lease: Missouri

Residential Lease: Montana

Residential Lease: Nebraska

Residential Lease: Nevada

Residential Lease: New Hampshire

Residential Lease: New Jersey

Residential Lease: New Mexico

Residential Lease: New York

Residential Lease: North Carolina

Residential Lease: North Dakota

Residential Lease: Ohio

Residential Lease: Oklahoma

Residential Lease: Oregon

Residential Lease: Pennsylvania

Residential Lease: Rhode Island

Residential Lease: South Carolina

Residential Lease: South Dakota

Residential Lease: Tennessee

Residential Lease: Texas

Residential Lease: Utah

Sublease: Oklahoma

Sublease: Oregon

Sublease: Pennsylvania

Sublease: Rhode Island

Sublease: South Carolina

Sublease: South Dakota

Sublease: Tennessee

Sublease: Texas

Sublease: Utah

Sublease: Vermont

Sublease: Virginia

Sublease: Washington

Sublease: West Virginia

Sublease: Wisconsin

Sublease: Wyoming

Tenant Employment Verification

Tenant Information Sheet

Tenant Move-Out Letter

Tenant Payment Record

Tenant Reference Check

Tenant's Notice to Terminate Tenancy

10-Day Notice to Quit: Arizona

10-Day Notice to Remedy Breach or Terminate: Arizona

10-Day Notice to Repair: Oklahoma

10-Day Notice to Vacate: Missouri

Termination Notice: Maine

3-Day Notice of Nonpayment of Rent: New Mexico

3-Day Notice of Substantial Violation of Rental Agreement: New Mexico

30-Day Notice of Violation: Maryland

30-Day Notice to Quit: New Hampshire

3-Day Notice to Quit: California

3-Day Notice to Quit: Idaho

3-Day Notice to Quit: Montana

3-Day Notice to Quit: Utah

3-Day Notice to Repair or Quit: California

3-Day Notice to Repair or Quit: Idaho

3-Day Notice to Repair or Quit: Montana

3-Day Notice to Repair or Quit: Utah

Unconditional Quit Notice

Unconditional Quit Second Notice

Violation of Pet Policy Letter

Waiver of Landlord's Claim to Annexed Fixtures

Waterbed Agreement-Addendum to Rental Agreement

APPENDIX D

Associations and Other Resources

Over the past decade, the world of information has changed considerably, particularly for real estate investors. Today, the Internet has created a wealth of property search and management resources that puts individuals in control of information as never before.

Web resources are spread throughout this book, but here is a summary of some of the most useful real estate investment sites you can find on the Web:

Associations

National Association of Realtors
www.realtor.org
National Association of Housing Cooperatives
www.coophousing.org

Construction Assistance

RS Means® Quick Cost Calculator
www.rsmeans.com/calculator/index.asp
Hanley Wood
(Provider of specialized paid reports on specific home renovation
and construction projects)
www.hanleywood.com

Credit Sites

FICO® Credit Score
www.myfico.com

Economic Information

UCLA Anderson Forecast
http://uclaforecast.com
U.S. Census Bureau Census of Housing
www.census.gov/hhes/www/housing/census/histcensushsg
.html

Financial/Tax Planning

The Financial Planning Association
www.fpanet.org
National Association of Fee-Only Financial Planners
ww.napfa.org
U.S. Securities and Exchange Commission EDGAR database
www.sec.gov/edgar.shtml
Federation of Exchange Accommodators 1031 Exchange information
www.1031.org/

Foreclosure Information

RealtyTrac.com
www.realtytrac.com
Foreclosure.com
www.foreclosure.com

For Sale by Owner (FSBO) Information

ForSalebyOwner.com
www.forsalebyowner.com
BuyOwner.com
www.buyowner.com

HomeKeys.com
www.homekeys.com

Mortgage Trends

HSH Associates, Financial Publishers
www.hsh.com

Journals

CNNMoney.com
http://money.cnn.com/real_estate
Bankrate.com
www.bankrate.com

APPENDIX E

Glossary of Real Estate Terms

Please note: The terms described below are just part of a much larger Real Estate Dictionary available to readers of this book at www.completelandlord.com.

A

Abandonment Voluntarily giving up one's right and interest in a particular property either by refusing to honor the obligations of that property (e.g., mortgage, taxes, and upkeep) or by declaring an intention to do so in the future. One reason for just walking away from an investment might be that the owner has lost his or her job, can no longer afford the fixed expenses of the house or condominium, or has discovered that the value of the house, if it were sold, is less than the outstanding balance on the mortgage.

Abatement A reduction or decrease in the value of a property that affects its market value or the amount of rent that may be charged to a tenant. Abatement usually occurs as the result of a discovery of something negative about the property (e.g., the roof must be replaced, the furnace will not make it through the winter, there is serious termite damage to the house) that decreases its worth and the price or rent it can command or, in the case of a sale in progress, affects the price already agreed on by the buyer and seller. The term can also refer to a decrease in the local government's valuation of a property, which in turn leads to lower taxes.

Absentee Owner/Landlord An owner of a property who lives somewhere else and is not directly in control of that property. Tenants not only occupy the property but, if the owner has not appointed an agent, may also manage the property on the absentee owner's behalf on a day-to-day basis.

Absorption Rate The number of properties within a property development (e.g., a tract of land on which houses are being built; a building in which apartments are being converted to condominiums) that can be sold in a certain market within a particular time. Because the owner/buyer has probably borrowed money to fund the development and is paying interest on that money, he or she must factor in interest costs as part of the basic expenses.

Abut To share a common (property) boundary or even share a portion of that boundary.

Acceptance A positive (and voluntary) response to an offer or counteroffer for a property that includes price and terms. This positive response creates a binding agreement between the buyer and seller. Acceptance may be conditional (i.e., based on certain events taking place). For example, in buying a new residence, the buyer may make his or her offer conditional on the sale of his or her current home within a certain number of months.

Access The right to enter a property. This may be restricted to certain times and to certain categories of people (e.g., those who read gas or electric meters or deliver the mail).

Accessory Building A structure on a property (e.g., a garage; a garden shed) that serves a specific purpose for the home or main building.

Accrued Interest Interest that has been earned but not yet claimed by the person to whom it is owed.

Acknowledgment A written declaration by a person executing a legal document, given before someone authorized to accept such oaths (usually a notary public), stating that the person signing the document did so voluntarily.

Acre A land area that is equal to 43,560 square feet. Property, particularly farm property, is often described in acres.

Act of God Damage to property caused by natural forces such as rain, lightning, floods, mudslides, snow, forest fires, or earthquakes.

Action to Quiet Title A legal action started by one of the parties to a dispute involving the ownership of a property—for the purpose of settling competing claims and establishing one clear legal title to the property.

Actual Age The years a building has been in existence (i.e., its chronological age). Its effective age is a more subjective judgment; it reflects the condition of the building (i.e., how well it has been maintained). Two houses on the same street may both have been constructed 50 years ago (i.e., their actual age), but one, because of upkeep and renovation, may look almost new, whereas the other, because of neglect, may look much older than its chronological age (i.e., its effective age).

Actual Cash Value A term used in the insurance industry to describe the valuation of a building. It is determined by subtracting the decrease in value caused by such factors as age and wear and tear from the actual current cost of replacing the building.

Addendum Something added to a document (e.g., lease, contract, purchase agreement) that then forms part of it. May be used to add some provision to the original document or to clarify some aspect of that original document.

Additional Principal Payment Making an additional payment on a mortgage. With a monthly mortgage payment of $2,000, the interest portion may be $1,750 and the principal portion may be $250. If the lender offers this sort of provision (and most do), the borrower may opt occasionally to pay an additional amount to reduce the principal (i.e., the amount owed) by more than the fixed amount of $250. Sometimes borrowers who have acquired a sum of money through means such as the sale of another asset, a tax refund, or an inheritance choose to make a substantial one-time payment of this kind. The advantage is that the total interest over the life of the loan is reduced.

Adjustable-Rate Mortgage (ARM) Also called a variable-rate mortgage. This kind of loan has an interest rate that is determined by some outside index, such as the federal prime rate or the interest paid on government bonds. This kind of mortgage is most popular when this rate is lower, especially when it is much lower, than the interest on a fixed-rate mortgage would be. People who choose these kinds of mortgage are hoping that the adjustable rate will remain below the fixed rate for a long time—or at least until their income improves. The savings in interest on an ARM, at least in the short term, can be substantial.

Adjustments Anything that, at closing, changes the value of the property (e.g., taxes overpaid or underpaid by the seller, fuel for several months stored on the premises and provided to the buyer, rent collected from tenants for the following month). A statement of adjustments is presented by the closing officer to the buyer or seller.

Administrator A person appointed by a court to oversee the estate of an individual who has died intestate (i.e., without leaving a will).

Adverse Possession A method of claiming ownership (i.e., title) to a piece of land that is formally owned by another, by occupying it. Most governments allow such a claim, provided it is not disputed by the title-holder and the claimant has occupied the land for a certain period (the required period varies by jurisdiction).

Affidavit of Title The seller's statement that the title (i.e., proof of ownership) is valid, can be sold, and is subject to no defects except those set out in the agreement of sale.

After-Tax Cash Flow The net profit of an income property after direct costs (e.g., interest on the mortgage, taxes, maintenance) have been subtracted.

After-Tax Proceeds The net proceeds from the sale of a property; that is, the sale price less the legal fees and expenses, the Realtor's commission, any taxes paid, and so on.

Agent Anyone (albeit usually a real estate agent) who is authorized by a buyer or seller of property to act on that person's behalf in any dealings with third parties. The third party may rely on the agreement and assurances of the agent as being binding on the person represented.

Amortization Schedule A statement of the payments to be made on an amortized mortgage loan. This statement generally shows the date and amount of each payment, the portions of each payment that will be applied to interest and to principal, and the balance (of principal) still outstanding on the loan after the payment has been made.

Annual Debt Service The amount required to service a loan in any given year; that is, the interest that must be paid to keep the loan current.

Annual Mortgagor Statement A document that is sent each year, usually at the end of the year, by the lender to the borrower regarding a mortgage loan. It details amounts paid for principal, interest, and (if the mortgage company pays the borrower's property taxes) taxes paid; it also notes the amount still owed on the mortgage.

Annual Percentage Rate (APR) The total cost of a loan (i.e., of borrowing the money to buy a property) in any given year expressed as a percentage of a loan amount (e.g., 6.5 percent). It includes compounded interest. The lender (i.e., the institution or person that holds the mortgage) is required by the Federal Truth-in-Lending Act to disclose the APR to the borrower.

Appraisal An estimate of the value of a property on a certain date, usually provided by a qualified appraiser, after both an inspection of the property and a comparison of that property with other comparable properties that have recently been sold.

Appreciation The increase in value of a property over time. This increase can be the result of many factors, such as inflation, increased demand for property resulting from low interest rates, the condition of the market, or the gentrification of a particular area.

Arrears Money that, under an amortization schedule, was not paid when it was due. The mortgagee is usually given the chance to make up the arrears. If he or she fails to do so, the mortgage holder can call in the loan (i.e., demand that it be paid in full).

As Is/As-Is Agreement The situation in which a property is accepted by the buyer (or tenant) in the condition existing at the time of the sale or lease; the seller (or lessor) is released from any liability after closing. Most agreements of sale contain such a provision.

Asking Price The amount at which a property is offered, by a seller, for sale. This price may change as a result of negotiations between the buyer and seller. In a tight market, a good property in a desirable location may bring more than the initial asking price as a result of bidding by numerous potential buyers.

Assessed Value The value placed on a property by a tax assessor for the purpose of determining property taxes.

Assign To transfer interest in a property. An elderly person might decide to transfer ownership in a piece of land to children who might be more likely to develop it.

Attached Housing Two or more houses, occupied by different people, that have a common wall (e.g., townhouses).

Auction Selling property to the highest bidder at a public sale. Auctions are often used to sell property that has been foreclosed on or property that has failed to sell in the marketplace.

B

Back-Title Letter/Certificate In states in which lawyers are required to examine title for title insurance purposes, this document is given to the attorney by the title insurance company to certify the condition of a title as of a certain date.

Backup Contract A secondary offer (from a potential buyer) for a property on which an offer from another buyer has already been made. This contract will come into effect if the first offer is not accepted or is withdrawn.

Balance The amount of principal still outstanding on a mortgage or other loan at any given time.

Balloon Mortgage A mortgage loan repaid in fixed, periodic (probably monthly) payments until a given date. On that date, either the balance of the loan becomes due in one large payment or the amount of the payments rises significantly.

Balloon Payment The final payment that pays off a balloon mortgage.

Base Rent The set rent paid by a tenant and to which can be added additional fees as set out in the lease (e.g., for upkeep, utilities).

Bedroom Community An area that includes mainly housing (residential or rental) and very few businesses. The term usually refers to a commuter town or suburb whose residents work in the central city or in more economically diverse suburbs.

Bi-Level Premises that are on two levels; commonly refers to a house but can also refer to an apartment or condominium unit. Also called split-level.

Bill of Sale A document that certifies that, in return for a certain price, ownership of property has passed from the seller to the purchaser.

Bi-Weekly Mortgage A mortgage in which one half of the monthly payment is made every 2 weeks. With this kind of mortgage, 26 payments will be made in a year; the extra monthly payment that is made each year reduces the duration of the mortgage and the total amount of interest the borrower will ultimately pay. Many people find such plans to be a fairly painless way to reduce the principal on a mortgage more quickly.

Blueprint Construction plans, usually prepared by an architect.

Borrower (mortgagor) A person who receives money from a lender to buy property, in exchange for a written promise to repay that money with interest. The borrower also accepts the lender's lien on that property until the debt is paid in full.

Boundary The legally determined edge or limit of a property.

Breach of Contract In law, the failure to live up to the terms of any contract.

Broker Refers to two kinds of agents: a mortgage broker, who brings potential borrowers together with potential lenders; and a real estate broker, who brings buyers together with sellers. Real estate broker is a professional designation; it requires training and licensing.

Building Permit A permit issued by a local government to allow a builder to construct a building or to make improvements to existing structures.

Building Restrictions Rules in the building code (e.g., zoning restrictions) that control the size, placement, design, and materials of new construction.

Buyer's Broker/Agent A real estate agent who represents the potential buyer. Agents commonly represent the seller, but potential buyers increasingly are engaging real estate agents to watch out for their interests also.

Buyer's Market A market in which there is more property for sale than there are buyers available to purchase it. This situation usually causes the value of available property to decrease. It most commonly occurs in overbuilt markets or when a poor economy results in fewer buyers being present in the marketplace.

Buy-Sell Offer An offer by one owner to buy out the interests of another owner or partner.

C

Cancellation Clause A clause in a contract, such as a mortgage, that sets forth the conditions under which each party may cancel or terminate the agreement.

Cap A limit. A cap is important in adjustable-rate mortgages, where it represents the limit on how high payments may go or how much the interest rate may change within a given period or over the life of the mortgage.

Capital Gain An increase in the value of capital property (i.e., property other than a principal residence) on which tax is payable, usually upon sale of the property.

Capital Loss A decrease in the value of capital property (i.e., property other than a principal residence), which the owner may use against capital gains or against regular income when paying his or her taxes, depending on the tax rules.

Cash Flow Net earned income from an income property after all the expenses of holding and carrying the property are paid or factored in. Also called cash throw-off.

Cash Reserve The amount of money a buyer of a property still has on hand after she or he has made a down payment and paid out the fees of closing. Some lenders ascertain that such a reserve exists (commonly, the equivalent of two mortgage payments) before granting a mortgage.

Cash Sale The sale of a property for cash; no mortgage or other financing is involved.

Caveat Emptor (Latin: Let the Buyer Beware). A legal maxim suggesting that the buyer of any property takes a risk regarding the condition of the property, and that it is the responsibility of the buyer to determine the condition before the purchase is completed. Many states now have laws that place more responsibility for disclosure on the seller and the real estate broker. Potential buyers should always check on their rights with their real estate broker.

CC&Rs Abbreviated term for covenants, conditions, and restrictions, which are the obligations of any real estate contract.

Certified General Appraiser Someone who is licensed, after training, to appraise the value of property (qualification requirements can vary, depending on the particular jurisdiction).

Certified Home Inspector (CHI) Someone who is licensed, after training, to inspect and report on the physical condition of property (qualification requirements may vary, depending on the particular jurisdiction).

Certified Property Manager (CPM) Someone who has met the requirements of the Institute of Real Estate Management to manage property. The Institute is an affiliate of the National Association of Realtors.

Certified Residential Appraiser (CRA) Someone who has met the licensing requirements to appraise the value of residential property only. See **certified general appraiser**.

Certified Residential Broker (CRB) Someone who has met the requirements of the Realtors National Marketing Institute to be an agent or broker for residential properties. The Realtors National Marketing Institute is affiliated with the National Association of Realtors.

Certified Residential Specialist (CRS) Someone who has met the requirements of the Realtors National Marketing Institute, which is affiliated with the National Association of Realtors. A CRS must have successfully completed an educational program, have an acceptable level of residential sales experience, and already be a graduate of the Real Estate Institute.

Chattel A word not used much in common speech but often used in real estate documents to describe personal property that is part of the property but is not fixed to the land or to a building. This is different from a fixture, which is part of the land or building. A homeowner's dining room table and chairs are a form of chattel; the chandelier above the table, which is secured to the ceiling, is a fixture. Fixtures are commonly included in the sale of a property, whereas chattels usually are not unless they are itemized in the agreement of sale.

Clear Title Property for which the title is free of competing claims, liens, or mortgages. Also called free and clear.

Closing The final procedure in any real estate transaction in which the parties to the transaction (or their representatives) meet to execute documents, exchange funds and complete the sale (and, if a mortgage is involved, the loan). A closing typically takes place at the offices of a title company.

Closing Costs Expenses, usually those of the buyer, that are over and above the cost (i.e., the sale price) of the property itself, such as legal fees, mortgage application fees, taxes, appraisal fees, title registration fees, and so on.

Code Laws or regulations that are drawn up (often by the government) to cover a particular aspect of life in a municipality or state (e.g., a building code, a traffic code).

Commission The amount paid to a real estate agent or broker as compensation for services rendered in the purchase, sale, or rental of property. The amount is usually a percentage of the sale price or the total rental.

Commitment/Commitment Letter A written promise, by a lender or insurance company, to make a loan or insure a loan for a specified amount and on specified terms.

Commitment Fee The fee that may be charged by a potential lender in return for the lender's promise to provide a mortgage to a potential borrower when that person finds property he or she wishes to buy.

Common-Area Assessments A periodic charge (usually monthly) that is levied against owners in a condominium complex. These fees are used by the condominium owners' association to pay for the maintenance of common areas in the building. Some assessments also include fees for utilities such as central heating or air conditioning. Also known as common-element fees or assessments.

Comparables A way of establishing the market value of a particular property in which another property that has recently been sold and is similar in location, size, condition, and amenities to the property in question is used as a guide to establish the asking price.

Condition(s) Requirements in a real estate purchase agreement that must be fulfilled before the agreement becomes firm and binding. If the conditions are not fulfilled, the agreement will usually be regarded as canceled and any deposit will be returned to the buyer.

Condominium A structure comprising two or more units in which the units are individually owned but the remainder of the property (i.e., the land, buildings, amenities) is owned in common. The maintenance of these common areas is supervised by the condominium corporation, in which each unit owner retains a share and has voting rights.

Consumer Reporting Agency or Bureau The source to which lenders turn for the credit history of any applicant for a loan. Also called a credit bureau.

Contingency A condition that must be fulfilled before a contract can become firm and binding. For example, the sale of a house may depend on whether the potential buyer can obtain financing.

Contract An agreement between two or more persons (or entities) that creates (or modifies) a legal relationship. In real estate, a contract is usually an offer for property and an acceptance of that offer (e.g., an agreement of sale).

Conversion (1) Renovation of an apartment to a condominium unit, or (2) the improper taking of another person's property for one's own use (e.g., moving into a person's vacation home and living there while the person is away).

Co-op Abbreviated term for cooperative, a form of ownership in which the occupiers of individual units in a building have shares in the cooperative corporation that owns the entire property. Co-ops are still popular in large U.S. cities, such as New York and Chicago, but condominiums are the more usual form of apartment ownership in most U.S. cities and suburbs.

Co-tenancy A situation in which more than one person owns a piece of property. Title is held by the owners in one of two ways: (1) as joint tenants, where each tenant owns the land equally and, in the event of the death of one of the tenants, his or her surviving co-tenant(s) will continue to own title equally by right of survivorship; or (2) as tenants in common, where each owner owns a specific portion of the property and may sell, mortgage, or bequeath that interest to a third party without the consent of the other owners.

Counteroffer A response to an offer. If a prospective buyer makes an offer to purchase a property (i.e., offers a price for that property), the seller may do one of three things: (1) accept the offer; (2) reject the offer outright; or (3) suggest an alternative. For example, the listed or advertised price of a condominium is $350,000 and the prospective buyer offers $325,000. The seller makes a counteroffer of $340,000. By suggesting this alternative, the seller is legally regarded as having rejected the buyer's original offer. The buyer in turn may also counteroffer (e.g., suggest a price of $330,000).

Covenant A promise contained in a contract or agreement. In real estate, this promise may be implied; it may already be covered by local or national laws.

Credit Limit The maximum amount that an individual can borrow to buy property. This amount is set by the lender after an examination of the individual's credit history/credit report.

D

Debt-Equity Ratio A comparison of what is owed on a property with its equity (i.e., the current market value of the property less the amount owed on the mortgage or loan).

Debt Financing The purchase of a property using any kind of credit rather than paying cash.

Decree of Foreclosure A court decree made when a borrower is seriously in default on a mortgage and the lender decides that the borrower will not (or cannot) pay. The decree declares the amount outstanding on the delinquent mortgage and orders the sale of the property to pay off the mortgage. The lender is then repaid to the extent possible (sales that result from foreclosure do not necessarily achieve full market value of the property).

Deed The legal instrument by which title to (i.e., ownership of) property is conveyed from one owner to another when a sale occurs.

Default The failure to make mortgage payments in full or on time or to live up to any other obligations of the mortgage agreement.

Defective Title Ownership that is not "clean" (i.e., subject to a competing claim or claims). Another meaning is ownership obtained by fraud.

Deferred Interest Interest that is not paid as it is incurred but instead is added to the loan's principal.

Deferred Maintenance This term refers to a property that has not been adequately maintained. Its condition, and therefore its value, is depreciating.

Delivery Turning over any legal document, particularly a deed, to another party, and in doing so making it legally nonrevocable.

Demand Loan A kind of loan that stipulates no fixed date for repayment but is due in full (i.e., principal with accumulated interest) if the lender asks for payment.

Deposit Money paid up front by a buyer to guarantee that she or he will actually complete a transaction to buy a particular property—in effect, it is a guarantee to the seller that the seller may remove the property from the market (i.e., the sale is "firm"). If the buyer later fails to complete the transaction, she or he generally loses the deposit. Also called earnest money.

Depreciation The decrease in value of a property over time, which can also lead to a reduction in the owner's taxes (i.e., a capital loss).

Designated Real Estate Broker An individual who has a real estate broker's license and who is appointed by a corporation or institution to oversee all of its real estate activities.

Designated Real Estate Instructor (DREI) Anyone who has met the requirements of the Real Estate Educators' Association and may therefore teach courses in real estate practice.

Detached Single-Family Home A freestanding house; that is, a house that does not share walls with another house and is designed to house just one family. Most houses in the United States are of this type.

Deterioration The effects of time and wear and tear on a property, or neglect of that property, which causes its value to decrease unless some action is taken to counteract and correct these effects.

Developer (1) A builder, most commonly someone who constructs a commercial complex or a residential subdivision, or (2) an entrepreneur who prepares raw land for construction, then in turn sells the lots to one or more builders so that they may build on the land.

Disclosure In some U.S. jurisdictions, the seller of a property must provide a written statement to the buyer listing those defects in the property of which the seller is aware. For example, the seller may know that the roof of the property needs to be replaced, but may be unaware that there is severe termite damage to the property. Also called vendor's disclosure.

Distress The right of a landlord or lender to sell the real or personal property of a tenant or borrower to pay for arrears in rent or loan payments.

Donor Someone who does one of the following things: offers a gift, makes a bequest, gives someone power of attorney, or settles property in a trust for another's benefit.

Doubtful Title Ownership of land or property that is questioned because of a seemingly equal claim on that land or property.

Down Payment The amount of money provided by the buyer toward the total price of the property (not including fees, taxes, or other costs). In general, the down payment plus the principal of the mortgage equals the purchase price. The down payment is customarily cash paid by the buyer from his or her own funds—as opposed to that part of the purchase price financed by a lender. A down payment amount that is common in the United States is 20 percent of the total purchase price. However, if the borrower agrees to insure this part of the mortgage, some lenders will accept a 10 percent down payment.

Downzoning A reduction in the density, under zoning bylaws, that is allowed by the local municipality for a certain property or neighborhood.

Duplex A single building that includes two separate living units. Also, an apartment or condominium unit that has two floors.

E

Encumbrance Any right, lien, or charge attached to and binding on a property. An encumbrance can affect the owner's ability or right to sell that property until such time as it is removed.

Equal Credit Opportunity Act A U.S. law guaranteeing that people of all races, ages, genders, and religions must have an equal chance to borrow money.

Equity The market value of a property, less the debts of that property. Likely debts include the principal and accumulated interest on the mortgage, unpaid taxes, and a home equity loan.

Escalator Clause Part of a net lease. This is a provision that allows the landlord to increase the rent payable if certain costs of the building increase, such as maintenance or utilities.

Escape Clause A provision in a contract that allows one or more of the parties involved to end the contract if certain events occur. For example, a potential buyer of a house may stipulate in the sale agreement that the agreement comes into effect only if the buyer is able to sell his or her current residence by the anticipated closing date.

Escrow In real estate, the delivery of a deed by the seller to a third party (i.e., the escrow agent), to be delivered to the buyer at a certain time, usually the closing date. In some states, all instruments having to do with the sale (including the funds) are delivered to the escrow agent for dispersal on the closing date.

Eviction A court action to remove an individual from the possession of real property, most commonly the removal of a tenant.

Evidence of Title A document that establishes ownership to property, most commonly a deed.

F

Fair Credit Reporting Act A federal law that protects consumers by establishing procedures whereby they can correct errors on credit reports; it gives consumers specific rights in dealing with credit-reporting agencies.

Fair Market Value The price that is likely to be agreed on by a buyer and seller for a specific property at a specific time. This price is typically arrived at by considering the sales prices of comparable properties in the area, taking into consideration any special features of or upgrades to the property in question.

Federal Truth in Lending Act A U.S. federal law that requires lenders to disclose all the terms of a loan arrangement (e.g., a mortgage) to the borrower in a specific, understandable way.

Fee Simple The best title to a property that is available—ownership that is not subject to dispute.

Fees (1) Fees that are charged for services provided by a real estate professional such as an appraiser or property inspector, or (2) the service charges that a borrower is required to pay a lender in return for making a loan (these fees are either charged at the outset or held back from the mortgage).

Finance Charge The entire cost of a loan or mortgage, including the principal and interest charged over the life of the loan, appraisal and application fees, and title insurance fees and recording fees.

Fire and Extended-Coverage Insurance An undertaking by an insurance company to compensate an owner of a property for a specific kind of damage to that property, such as damage caused by a hurricane. This kind of property insurance is important to a property owner in Florida, the Gulf Coast states, or the shoreline of the Eastern Seaboard.

Firm Commitment A promise from a lender to lend a potential borrower a specific amount of money (on specific terms) to be secured against a particular property—in other words, a promise by the lender to give the potential borrower a mortgage.

First Mortgage A mortgage that, when registered, is the first to be able to claim payment from any sale proceeds. Often, owners of property take out a second mortgage, usually to "tap" some of the equity in their property. Such mortgages are paid, on a sale, only after the first mortgage has been paid.

Fixed Expenses These are the certain costs of owning and operating a property. The cost of painting a house is not a fixed expense but the property tax on that house is.

Flip The practice whereby a property is purchased in the hope that it can be sold quickly for a higher price. Often refers to the practice whereby someone reserves (with a comparatively small reservation fee) a condominium unit in a building that is being constructed (or being converted from apartments); by the time the property is ready, but before the purchaser has to go through a closing, the condominium has increased in value and the purchaser can sell it for a high price, having invested only the amount necessary to "reserve" the property.

Floating Rate The rate of interest charged on an adjustable-rate mortgage. This rate usually is set according to a specified index or is tied to the national prime rate. For example, a loan set at *prime plus 2 percent* will carry an interest rate of 7 percent if the prime rate is 5 percent.

Forced Sale A sale that is not voluntary on the part of the seller, such as a sale to satisfy a pressing debt or a sale resulting from bankruptcy. The selling price, in such a sale, is often less than true market value, sometimes considerably so.

Foreclosure A proceeding that is usually instigated by a lender, in court or not, to cancel all rights and title of an owner of a particular property when that owner has defaulted on payment of a mortgage. The purpose of the lender's action is to claim the title, so that the property can be sold to satisfy the debt still outstanding on the mortgage.

Gross Income The total of a person's earnings from his or her job plus any other income (e.g., interest income or dividends on stock) in a given period, before that person's expenses are deducted.

H

Habitable A dwelling or property that is acceptable for human occupancy; that is, it is not derelict and meets standards of decency.

Handyman's Special A property that requires substantial work to bring it up to normal standards. Such a property is often sold at a lower price than it would be if it were in excellent repair.

Hazard Insurance A policy on property (or on property improvements) that covers damage by natural causes, such as fire or flooding.

High-Ratio Mortgage A mortgage in which the amount of money borrowed is 75 percent (or more) of the purchase price. The lender on such a mortgage usually requires the sort of insurance that is provided by various U.S. government agencies as a guarantee of the lender's risk in making the mortgage.

High-Rise A tall apartment or commercial building that meets one or both of two criteria: (1) it is taller than six stories, and/or (2) it is tall enough to make an elevator a necessity rather than a convenience.

Hold-Harmless Clause A clause in a contract in which one party releases another from legal liability for a stated risk. For example, a person who wishes to rent an apartment from a landlord may agree to sign a lease only if that lease includes a hold-harmless clause absolving the tenant from having to make any repairs that become necessary during the tenancy. Also known as a save-harmless clause.

Holding Over The action of a tenant who continues to occupy premises after his or her lease has expired. Also known as overholding.

Home Equity Line of Credit A kind of loan that is increasingly popular. It is secured against the equity in a property. The borrower may borrow against that equity to a certain percentage of that equity's value and then, on a monthly basis, make payments of interest only or interest plus a portion of the equity borrowed, as desired. Many such loans have a time limit (i.e., the borrower must pay back the loan, if it is not already paid back, at some time in the future). Such a loan, which is in effect a second mortgage, must be paid back immediately if the property is sold. Also known as a revolving loan.

Home Inspector Someone who offers his or her services as an examiner of the physical condition of property. Qualifications for this profession differ between jurisdictions.

Homeowner's Insurance Liability coverage that provides for both loss and damage to property. Most mortgage lenders require this kind of insurance of borrowers, and many lenders require evidence that the policy has been renewed each year.

Housing Affordability Index An analysis by the National Association of Realtors, issued on a monthly basis, of the ability of the average-income family in the United States to afford a mortgage on the average-priced home, after making a 20 percent down payment.

Housing Expense Ratio A figure obtained by comparing a family's monthly gross income with the costs of their home (i.e., the principal and interest on a mortgage plus the cost of upkeep).

Housing Starts An economic indicator: the number of dwelling units (i.e., houses, apartments, and condominium units) on which construction is begun in a designated area in a prescribed period.

I

Improvements Any permanent structure or other development (usually buildings, but also streets, sewers, and utilities) that enhances the value of what was formerly vacant land.

Income Property Any property developed (or purchased) specifically to produce income for its owner, such as an apartment building.

Independent Appraisal An estimate of the value of a property in which the appraiser has no interest in the property (e.g., is not a representative of the potential lender).

Independent Contractor A person who is hired to do building or renovation work for another person but is neither an employee nor an agent of that other person, such as a contractor who works for a fee.

Initial Interest Rate The interest rate being charged on a mortgage on the day that it is first signed.

Installment Any regular, periodic payment, such as the monthly payment on a mortgage.

Insurance A contract in which one party (the insurer) agrees to indemnify another (the insured) against possible losses under specific conditions. Such conditions may include compensation of the insured for loss of job and income, in which case the insurer would pay the insured's debts, including mortgage payments, and compensation of the insured for any damage to the insured's property caused by natural phenomena (e.g., fire, storms).

Insured Mortgage A mortgage that is insured against loss to the lender in the event that the borrower defaults. It usually covers both the mortgage balance and the costs of foreclosure. This type of insurance is provided by such government agencies as the FHA or VA, as well as by independent insurance companies.

Interest (1) A person's legal right to property, or (2) the cost of borrowing money for any purpose, such as to buy property, charged as a percentage of the outstanding balance owed.

Interest-Only Mortgage A type of mortgage that is increasingly popular in which the borrower pays only the interest and none of the principal during a certain period (e.g., three years, five years). After that, the borrower makes conventional payments containing both principal and interest for the remainder of the loan's term. Such mortgages are appealing to those who want initial payments on a mortgage to be as low as possible or those who expect the value of the property to rise very quickly, providing them with a profit without a substantial principal investment.

Interest Payment That portion of each periodic payment on a loan or mortgage (expressed in dollars, not as a percentage) that is allocated toward accrued interest as opposed to principal.

Interest Rate The amount that a borrower pays to service a loan (i.e., to use the borrowed money), usually expressed as a percentage.

Investment Property Real estate that is owned not for the purpose of residential occupation, but for the possibility that it will increase in value or that its use will provide a good income.

J

Joint Ownership Agreement A contract between two or more people who have an interest in the same property. It sets out their rights and obligations and may also set out the way in which the parties agree to manage the property.

Joint Tenancy/Tenants See co-tenancy.

Judgment A decision rendered by a court. If a monetary settlement is involved, it may become a lien on the property of the losing party.

Junk Fees A slang term for the extra and sometimes unnecessary services that a lender may charge for on a mortgage.

L

Landlord Also known as lessor. The owner of a property who allows another person (or persons) to occupy that property in return for periodic payments of rent. The amount of the rent payments and the terms and conditions of the rental are usually established by a lease.

Landscaping The act of modifying a landscape, as well as the components used in such modification, such as changes in grade, trees and shrubs, lawns, flowers, and other plantings. The object of landscaping is to create a more pleasing appearance for the property, and one of its incidental goals is to enhance the value of that property. Landscaping may accomplish that goal, particularly if it is extensive, professional, and pleasing to a potential buyer.

Late Charge A penalty fee charged by a lender when a borrower is late with a mortgage payment.

Lease with Option to Purchase A kind of lease in which the tenant (i.e., lessee) has the right (but not the obligation) to purchase the property during the term of the lease. Payments made under the lease (sometimes wholly and sometimes in part, depending on the lease agreement) may be credited against the purchase price; that is, they may be used as a down payment. This is an ideal arrangement for any potential buyer who lacks the financial means to make a down payment.

Leasehold Improvements An often complex proposition in which additions made by a tenant to rented premises may be removed by the tenant at the end of the lease if no damage to the premises results (see chattel). Fixtures present no problem in this instance, but chattels may.

Legal Description A description of property that is acceptable in a court of law (i.e., meets legal requirements).

Legal Residence (1) In the United States, it usually means street address, city, state, and zip code; (2) for a person abroad, it can mean country of residence.

Legal Title The rights of ownership that are conferred on a person when he or she purchases a piece of property. These rights may be defended against any other, competing interests.

Lender A general term referring to any individual or company that provides money to a borrower in return for periodic payments of principal and interest over time. In real estate, the term most often refers to a person (or institution) who offers a borrower a mortgage (i.e., loans the borrower the money to buy property) and places a lien on that property until the outstanding loan (i.e., the principal) and all the outstanding interest on that loan are paid.

Lessee The tenant under a lease; someone who leases property.

Lessor See landlord.

Letter of Intent A formal letter stating that a prospective buyer is interested in a property. This is not a firm offer and it creates no legal obligation. A potential buyer could issue such a letter to a seller of a particular property, indicating that the buyer intends to make an offer for that property.

Lien An encumbrance or legal claim against a property as security for payment of a debt, such as the lien involved in a mortgage.

Listing Agent/Broker The real estate professional who acts for the seller in marketing a property. This is not the same as the selling agent, which represents potential buyers. One agent may act in both capacities for a client (e.g., be responsible for selling a person's current residence, then help them find a new residence).

Loan-to-Value Ratio The difference between the appraised value of a property and the amount being loaned on a mortgage.

Location The factor often cited as the primary feature in determining the worth of a property—as in the expression "location, location, location!" It refers to the following phenomenon: if two very similar properties are located in two different areas within the same city or town and one of those areas is more convenient to the region's most popular amenities (e.g., shopping, entertainment) than the other, the property in the more desirable location will almost certainly be more expensive.

Lock or Lock-in (1) The commitment from a lender to guarantee a certain interest rate (or other loan feature) for a designated period, or (2) the restriction that a mortgage may not be prepaid by the borrower for a specific period.

Lock Period The period during which a lender guarantees a particular loan feature, usually the interest rate.

Lot In general, any portion or parcel of real estate (i.e., a measured section of land). Often refers to a portion of a subdivision.

Lot Line The legal boundaries of a property, shown on a survey of that property.

Low-Ball Offer A slang term meaning to offer a purchase price that is much lower than the asking price. Such offers, often lower than the appraised market value, are frequently made when a property has been on the market for a long time and potential buyers try to take advantage of pressure on the seller to sell.

M

Maintenance Costs The expense required to keep a property in a good state of repair.

Market Price The amount actually paid for a property. At the moment of sale, that amount is imagined to be its current valuation;

subsequently, the market price, depending on economic factors, either appreciates or depreciates.

Market Rent The amount that an owner can reasonably charge someone who wishes to lease a property. The determining factor is generally how much other landlords in the same market are charging for similar properties. Also known as economic rent.

Mechanic's and Materialman's Liens A claim against property. Any person who supplies materials (or labor) for a property and is not paid may file this kind of claim against the property. Also known as a construction lien.

Minimum Down Payment The smallest amount of money that a purchaser is allowed to provide toward the purchase price of a house under a lender's guidelines for a mortgage. Down payments on residential property in the United States for many years have typically been 20 percent of the property's purchase price. However, down payments of 10 percent or even 5 percent have become more common recently. With down payments of less than 20 percent, lenders usually require additional insurance on the mortgage. The borrower may cancel this insurance when the principal on the loan reaches 20 percent.

Monthly Housing Expense The total cost of maintaining a home each month, including the principal and interest on a mortgage, real estate taxes, and property (and possibly mortgage) insurance. This figure usually does not include maintenance or improvements, only fixed expenses.

Mortgage A loan usually granted for the purpose of allowing a borrower to purchase property. The loan is secured (i.e., guaranteed) by that property; in other words, the mortgage is registered on the title (i.e., the ownership record) as a claim on that property.

Mortgage Broker A middleman who brings borrowers together with potential lenders, thereby providing a service to borrowers who are not as informed about potential lending sources. Often, the broker collects a fee for this service from the chosen lender.

Mortgagee In a mortgage transaction, this is the lender—the bank, other institution (private or government), or person making the loan for property.

Mortgage-Loan Servicing The lender's actions in collecting mortgage payments and allocating those payments to principal, interest, and, if the mortgage so stipulates, an escrow account for subsequent payment of property taxes and insurance premiums.

Multiple Listing Service (MLS) A local service that is created and staffed by real estate professionals. It brings together all property listed for sale in a given area (e.g., a town and its surrounding area or a city and its suburbs) so that real estate agents and brokers can review all available properties on behalf of their clients. The MLS also governs commission splitting and other relations between agents. Licensed real estate professionals have access to the service.

Municipal Address The designation (i.e., the street address, city, state, and zip code) by which a property is known.

N

Negotiable A term that commonly refers to something that is assignable or transferable (i.e., something that is capable of being negotiated). In real estate, the term refers to the fact that the price of a property is often the result of a negotiation between the buyer and seller and that many of the charges on a home loan are also subject to negotiation.

Net Operating Income (NOI) The income from a property that is left after the costs of maintaining and servicing that property are subtracted.

No Bid The situation in which the Veterans' Administration chooses not to acquire a property in foreclosure when that property is in default, but instead opts to pay out the amount it has guaranteed (usually 60 percent of the principal).

No Money Down A slang term for the strategy of purchasing real estate using as little of the buyer's own money as possible. Can also refer to an uncommon kind of mortgage that requires very little or no down payment.

Nominal Loan Rate The interest rate stated in a loan agreement such as a mortgage.

Normal Wear and Tear Damage to a property that is the result of neither carelessness nor maliciousness but simply reasonable use and the passage of time.

Notice to Quit An announcement from a landlord to a tenant that the tenant has not followed the terms of the lease and must leave the property.

Nuisance A use of property that obviously interferes with the use and enjoyment of nearby properties (e.g., noise, fumes, aggressive behavior by pets). Such nuisances may be grounds for legal action by the people who are suffering from the nuisance.

O

Occupancy The physical possession of a building or property.

Offer A statement (either spoken or written) that informs one party of another's willingness to buy or sell a specific property on the terms set out in that statement. Once made, an offer usually must be accepted within a specific period (i.e., it is usually not open-ended). Once accepted, the offer by one party and the acceptance by the other are both regarded as binding.

On-Site Improvements Any work performed on a property that adds to its utility, value, or attractiveness.

Open-ended Mortgage A loan that allows the borrower to borrow further funds at a later date with the preparation (and registration) of an additional mortgage.

Open House A property that is available for public viewing during a set period. Potential buyers who wish to view the property do not need an appointment, and the real estate agent usually is present to conduct tours of the property and answer questions.

Open Listing A written authorization from a property owner to a real estate agent stipulating that the owner will pay the agent a commission if the agent presents an offer of specified price and terms. The agent does not, however, have an exclusive right to sell; in fact, the owner may have made the same arrangement with several agents, and only the successful agent will be paid the commission.

Option to Purchase Leased Property A clause in a rental agreement that allows the tenant the right to buy the leased property on terms and conditions that are also set out in the agreement.

Ordinary Repairs Repairs that are necessary to keep a property in good condition, as opposed to ordinary wear and tear.

Original Cost The purchase price of a property; the amount that was paid by the current owner.

Owner's Title Insurance A policy that protects a property owner from any defects in title that were not apparent at the time of purchase.

P

Package Mortgage A mortgage that is secured by the borrower's personal as well as real property.

Paper Profit An asset, such as property, that is known to have increased in value (e.g., because comparable assets have been sold and have achieved this value) but has not actually produced a profit because it has not been sold. Therefore, the profit remains speculative.

Parcel A general term meaning any piece of land.

Partial Interest Less than 100 percent ownership of a property.

Partial Release The release of a portion of property covered by a mortgage. For example, a developer of a subdivision of residential properties may obtain such a release as each house is sold and payment of a stated portion of the loan has been made.

Payment Cap A condition of some adjustable-rate mortgages in which the level to which a monthly payment can rise is limited to a certain amount.

Payment Change Date Under an adjustable-rate mortgage, the date on which the payment changes.

Permit A government body's written permission allowing changes to a particular property when such changes are regulated by that government body. For example, local municipalities normally require homeowners to apply for a permit if they wish to make substantial alterations to the outsides of their houses to make sure that these changes are not at variance with the bylaws covering the area in which the houses are located.

Personal Property Any property belonging to an individual that is not real property (i.e., not real estate).

Personal Residence A person's home; the place from which that person votes, pays taxes, and so on.

Plat A map dividing a parcel of land into lots, as in a subdivision.

Point An amount equal to 1 percent of the principal of a mortgage. This is a fee that is charged to a borrower by a lender for originating the mortgage. It is a loan service charge that must be paid up front when the mortgage goes into effect. Some lenders allow points to be added to the principal of the mortgage and paid over its lifetime.

Possession The state of being in control of property, regardless of ownership. Thus, possession may be either legal or "wrongful."

Power of Attorney An authority by which one person (the principal) designates another to act on her or his behalf in commercial transactions (e.g., signing a lease).

Preapproved Mortgage A commitment from a lender to provide a mortgage loan to a borrower on stated terms before the borrower has found a property to buy. Most real estate agents recommend that their clients who are potential buyers secure this kind of commitment because it allows them to make a firm offer when they find a desirable property; that is, they do not have to ask a seller to wait several weeks while they attempt to obtain financing. Sometimes sellers are unwilling to wait and potential buyers may lose property.

Prepayment Payment of all or part of the principal of a mortgage or loan before it is actually due.

Prequalification Completion of the mortgage application process before the borrower has found a property to buy as a way of establishing how much money the borrower is qualified to obtain in a mortgage.

Primary Lease The main lease on a property, to which any subleases are subordinate.

Prime Rate The most favorable interest rate charged by the largest commercial banks on short-term loans. Such loans usually are reserved for the lender's best clients. In real estate, the prime rate is not a rate that is actually charged on a mortgage, although adjustable-rate mortgages often use it as their index. Such mortgages may offer interest rates that are always two or three percentage points above the prime rate.

Principal (1) The person on whose behalf a real estate agent is acting, or (2) the amount of money borrowed (or still owed) on a loan, excluding interest.

Principal and Interest Payment (P&I) A periodic payment on a mortgage sufficient to pay off the accumulated interest (which typically accumulated over the previous month) and a portion of the principal.

Prospect A potential tenant, buyer, or seller, rather than someone who is in the process of leasing, buying, or selling.

Q

Qualified Buyer A potential purchaser who has been preapproved for a mortgage, usually to a certain limit.

Quit-Claim Deed A conveyance in which the person doing the conveying is stating that she or he has no interest in a particular property.

R

Real Estate The term for land and all fixtures to land, including buildings and improvements. Personal property is not usually considered real estate. A house is real estate, but the furniture in the house is not.

Real Estate Market The real estate activity (i.e., purchases and sales) in a particular area at a particular time.

Recording The act of entering a title (or titles) into the public records.

Redeem To bring mortgage payments up-to-date after a serious delinquency in making those payments, and after the lender has started default proceedings. Once a borrower redeems, the mortgage is regarded as back in good standing.

Redemption The process of canceling a title to property, such as what happens in a mortgage foreclosure or as the result of a tax sale of a property.

Redevelop To remove existing improvements (usually buildings) on a piece of land and replace them with new, more useful or more profitable improvements.

Refinance The situation when a borrower pays off one loan on a property and replaces it with another loan, often from the same lender. This is done most commonly when mortgage interest rates have decreased considerably from the rate the borrower is paying on the old mortgage. Thus, refinancing is a way for the borrower to reduce the amount of monthly mortgage payments.

Rehabilitate To restore or refurbish real estate.

Relocation Clause A condition in a lease that allows a landlord to move a tenant to a new unit, within the same building or elsewhere. The clause usually specifies that the new premises must be of the same standard and quality as the old premises from which the tenant is being moved.

Renegotiation An attempt to agree on new terms to an existing contract. In real estate, there are two common examples of renegotiation: (1) when the necessary repairs to a property as established by a home inspection are more extensive than the seller had announced or the buyer had expected, or (2) when the appraisal of a property establishes a value or market price considerably below the price on which the parties to the contract had agreed. In both cases, the buyer will wish to renegotiate the price of sale.

Renovate Another word for remodel, though it implies a much more extensive upgrade to the property.

Rent As a noun: Payments made by a tenant to a landlord for the right to occupy premises owned by the landlord. As a verb: The act of leasing premises from a landlord.

Required Cash The total amount of money needed to complete a real estate transaction. This may include a down payment on the purchase price, taxes, legal fees, and mortgage fees.

Rescind/Rescission To treat a property contract as ended or void; that is, to withdraw one's offer or acceptance of a contract. Rescission normally happens as a result of a breach of the contract by the other party to that contract.

Reserve Fund The fund maintained by a condominium corporation (or a cooperative) for future contingencies, such as unforeseen major structural repairs to the condominium building that are very expensive. A reserve fund is usually created by charging unit owners a monthly assessment that is slightly more than what is needed to cover the basic maintenance expenses of the building and placing the extra amount in the reserve fund.

Rezoning The reclassification of a property, or a particular district, from one kind of use to another. An area might be rezoned from commercial to residential, which would allow former office buildings to be converted into residential condominiums.

S

Sale Price The amount of money paid by the buyer to the seller for a particular property. Also known as purchase price.

Sales Associate/Salesperson A real estate professional who is employed by and works under a real estate broker.

Scheduled Mortgage Payment The periodic payment (usually monthly) that a borrower is obliged to pay on a loan. Depending on the terms of the loan, this payment may include amounts only for principal and interest or also for real estate taxes and insurance premiums.

Search A review of public records undertaken to investigate whether there are any problems with the title to a particular property.

Second Mortgage A mortgage that ranks after a first mortgage in priority. A single property may have more than one mortgage; each is ranked by number to indicate the order in which it must be paid. In the event of a default and therefore sale of the property, second and subsequent mortgages are paid in order only if there are funds left after payment of the first mortgage.

Secondary Market The marketplace where investors buy and sell existing mortgages. The purchasers of first mortgages include banks, government agencies, insurance companies, investment bankers, and independent investors. The original lender often sells mortgages in the secondary market so as to have an adequate supply of money available for new loans in the future.

Security Deposit Money paid by a tenant to a landlord, then held by the landlord to ensure that the tenant meets the obligations of the lease and does not damage the property. If the tenant does damage the property, the landlord may use part (or all) of the money to make the necessary repairs. In many jurisdictions, the landlord is required to pay interest on a security deposit.

Seller Financing An arrangement in which a seller agrees to receive payment of part or all of the purchase price over an extended period. The debt is registered on the title as a mortgage, and the seller acts as the lender, accepting monthly payments of principal and accumulated interest.

Seller's Market The situation that exists when demand for property exceeds the availability of property. In such situations, a seller may set a price for her or his property that is higher than its real market value.

Sever/Severance To divide one property from another so that each may be sold or used separately.

Simple Interest Interest payable on just the principal of a loan and not on any accumulated interest.

Single-Family Home/Residence/Unit A house or condominium unit designed for a single family.

Site A plot of land set aside for a specific use, such as for the construction of a new factory.

Soft Market The situation that exists when there is more property for sale than there are buyers to buy it; as a result, prices decrease. Also known as buyer's market.

Spec House A new house built before the builder has found a buyer.

Speculator Someone who buys property in the expectation that it will increase in value within a relatively short period and can then be sold at a profit.

Stamp Tax Charges that are levied by governments (usually the local municipality) on the transfer of ownership of property.

Starter Home/Condominium A small house or condominium unit that is usually inexpensive and is suitable for a first-time buyer. The assumption is that the buyer will build up equity in the property and then use the equity as a down payment on a larger dwelling.

Statutory Lien An involuntary lien on property created by law (e.g., a tax lien) and to which the owner need not agree. A mortgage, by contrast, is a voluntary lien on property.

Straight-Term Mortgage A mortgage that requires that the principal be paid in full at the maturity of the loan.

Subcontractor Someone who works under a general contractor or builder, such as a roofer, electrician, or plumber.

Subdivision The division of a single large parcel of land into smaller parcels (i.e., lots), which usually requires government approval. The term most commonly refers to a new urban or suburban housing development. A condominium is sometimes called a *one-lot subdivision*.

Sublease A rental contract between a tenant and someone who rents from that tenant.

Surplus Funds In an enforced sale of property (e.g., a foreclosure on a mortgage), any funds that are left over after the principal, interest, and penalties have been paid. Often, these surplus funds are paid to the borrower whose default provoked the sale.

Survey Usually a pictorial depiction of land, showing its boundaries and the improvements that have been made to it.

Surveyor A professional who is trained to prepare accurate surveys.

Survivorship Put simply, this is outliving others. Surviving joint tenants (see co-tenancy) have the right to take title to land they owned with a deceased joint tenant (i.e., they have the right of survivorship).

Sweat Equity A slang term for the improvements an owner makes to property through his or her own manual labor. Such improvements are expected to add to the value of the property.

T

Tangible Property Assets that have a physical existence that can be touched (e.g., real estate).

Tax A government levy against real property. If taxes are unpaid, the government may attach a lien to the property. Such liens are regarded as preeminent (i.e., they are given priority over mortgages).

Tax Base The assessed valuation of a piece of real property. This value is multiplied by the government's tax rate to determine the amount of property tax due.

Tax Foreclosure The process leading up to the sale of property to cover unpaid taxes.

Tax Lien A registered claim for the nonpayment of property taxes.

Tax Map A pictorial representation of properties in a particular municipality that provides information about those properties.

Tenancy at Will A kind of tenancy, created by written agreement, that allows the landlord to evict the tenant at any time. This kind of tenancy might come into effect for a condemned building for which the date of demolition has not been established by the owner or local government authority.

Tenancy in Common Ownership by more than one owner. This kind of ownership does not involve right of survivorship; the portion owned by the deceased becomes a part of the owner's estate.

Term Loan A loan that comes due on a particular date, regardless of whether the periodic payments have paid that loan in full.

Term of a Mortgage The period during which the loan contract is in effect and the borrower is making payments to the lender. The term is not necessarily the same as amortization (the period during which, if all payments are paid on time and in full, the loan will be paid). For example, a mortgage could be amortized over 30 years but have a term of 10 years; at the end of 10 years, the borrower must pay the balance of the loan in full or refinance the loan.

Title The evidence an owner has of his or her right of possession of property.

Title Company A corporation that sells insurance policies that guarantee the ownership of (and quality of title to) property. Also known as a title insurance company.

Title Insurance Policy An insurance policy that protects an owner (or lender) against loss from a defective title.

Total Debt Ratio The total costs of living for a person (e.g., debt, food, travel) over a particular period compared to her or his gross income. Also called debt-service ratio.

Total Interest Payments All the interest that will be paid over the life of a loan.

Townhouse A house that is not freestanding; it shares at least one wall with a neighboring house (or houses).

Tract A parcel of land. In some areas of the United States, the term also means subdivision.

Transfer Tax A state tax on the transfer of real property. In some areas of the United States, it is referred to as documentary transfer tax.

Trespass Entry onto (or even possession of) property that is owned by another person without the owner's consent.

Triple-Net Lease The sort of rental agreement that requires the tenant to pay all the operating costs of the premises.

U

Underwriter (1) A person who evaluates an application for a loan or an insurance policy, or (2) A company that insures another, such as a large title company (the underwriter) that sells insurance to a smaller title insurance company for all or a portion of the policies that the smaller company issues.

Undeveloped Land Land on which no work has been done to make it more useful or profitable. Also called raw land.

Unit A single dwelling in a larger complex. The term is most often used with regard to a condominium project. It refers to a unit (or, in a rental building, an apartment) that is reserved for the exclusive use of the owner, as opposed to the common areas (e.g., lobby, sun deck, laundry room) that are intended for the use of all the owners.

Unsecured Loan A loan that is valid (i.e., the lender has given the borrower the requested funds) but is not secured by any asset. Such loans are virtually unknown; an exception would be a case in which the lender knows the borrower well, has had extensive business dealings with the borrower, and believes that the loan will be repaid.

Up-Rent Potential An estimate of how much the rent on a particular property is likely to be raised over a given period. Such an estimate might be offered to a potential tenant as an inducement to sign a lease.

Urban Sprawl A slang term for the unplanned, often wasteful, and often unattractive growth of cities.

Utilities Services that are needed in any premises or dwelling (e.g., gas, electricity, sewer, water) and that the owner pays for separately from any payments on a loan. In some jurisdictions, arrears in payment of bills for utilities may create a lien on the property.

V

VA Loan A home loan offered to a military veteran that is guaranteed by the U.S. Department of Veterans' Affairs. It allows the veteran to buy a home with no money down.

Vacancy Rate A calculation, expressed as a percentage, of all the available rental units in a particular area and at a particular time that are not rented.

Vacate To move out of premises.

Valuation The estimation of the worth or likely sale price of land or property. Also known as appraisal.

Variable Expenses The operating costs of a property that are not fixed, such as heating costs, which can change dramatically depending on whether a winter is mild or severe.

Variance An "indulgence" granted by a local government authority to allow an unconventional use of property. This could be an exception granted to a homeowner that allows him or her to create a basement apartment for a sick relative in an area in which zoning bylaws ordinarily allow for only single-family homes.

W

Walk-Through Inspection An examination by the buyer of the property she or he is purchasing. The walk-through inspection usually takes place immediately before closing and is intended to assure the buyer that no changes have taken place (and no damage has been done) to the property since the buyer agreed to buy. It also reassures the buyer that fixtures and chattels included in the sale actually remain on the property.

Warranty A legally binding promise that is usually given at the time of sale in which the seller gives the buyer certain assurances as to the condition of the property being sold.

Wear and Tear The loss in value of a property that is caused by normal and reasonable use of that property. Usually, in a lease, a tenant is not responsible for normal wear and tear in the premises that tenant leases.

Wood-Frame Construction Buildings in which the internal elements (e.g., walls, floors) are all constructed of wood. This does not refer to the exterior of the building, which may be constructed of other materials, such as brick.

Work Order An edict from a local government body directing that certain work be done on a particular property to bring it into compliance with local regulations. Work orders usually are issued against property that has been allowed to become substandard or derelict.

Z

Zero Lot Line The construction of a building on the boundary lines of a lot. This usually is the front line (e.g., a store built directly to the sidewalk). In the older neighborhoods of some U.S. cities, it is also common for residences to be built up to the sidewalk.

Zone An area of a city (or county) that is set aside for a certain purpose, such as a commercial, residential, industrial, or agricultural zone.

INDEX

CLL Catalog Taken from Online Store at 6/08

CompleteLandlord.com Premium Membership Benefits

9 Key Components	Silver	Gold	Platinum
1. Property Management Solution℠	Up to 2 Units	Up to 10 Units	Up to 50 Units or more
Complete Tenant Tracking	Unlimited	Unlimited	Unlimited
General Ledger Accounting System	Unlimited	Unlimited	Unlimited
Management Reports	Unlimited	Unlimited	Unlimited
Dashboard	Unlimited	Unlimited	Unlimited
Resident Portal (Website)	Unlimited	Unlimited	Unlimited
2. Lease Creation Pro℠			
Customizable Forms and Letters	Unlimited	Unlimited	Unlimited
Leases & Rental Agreement	Unlimited	Unlimited	Unlimited
Rental Credit Application	Unlimited	Unlimited	Unlimited
Pre-Lease and Post-Lease Inspection List	Unlimited	Unlimited	Unlimited
Garage and Parking Space Agreement	Unlimited	Unlimited	Unlimited
Pet Agreement Addendum	Unlimited	Unlimited	Unlimited
Leases, Agreements, Notices	✓	✓	✓
Applications	✓	✓	✓
Disclosures	✓	✓	✓
Letters	✓	✓	✓
Inspection Forms	✓	✓	✓
Addendums, Warnings, Surveys	✓	✓	✓
5. Archives of Landlord Profit Letter and Quarterly Issues	✓	✓	✓
6. Access to CompleteLandlord.com Library Special Reports			
Rental Property Management Secrets for Landlords	✓	✓	✓
Complete Guide to Conducting Tenant Screenings		✓	✓
Eviction Secrets for Landlords		✓	✓
How to Buy Foreclosure Property			✓
Understanding Rental Property 1031 Exchanges for Landlords			✓
Streaming Webinar/Audio Conferences Hosted by Real Estate Experts			
Tax Planning Secrets for Landlords		✓	✓
Asset Protection Using LLCs			✓
7. Customer Care	✓	✓	✓
8. Content, Forms & Software Upgrades, Maintenance, Hosting, Storage, Multi-layer Security and Rental Unit Scaleability	Unlimited	Unlimited	Unlimited
9. Incremental rental unit additions	$2.00/unit/mo	$1.00/unit/mo	$0.30/unit/mo
Premium Membership Monthly Price	$9.97/mo	$19.97/mo	$29.97/mo
Premium Membership Annual Price	$97/yr	$197/yr	$297/yr
Annual Membership Savings vs. Monthly Membership	(Save $22.64)	(Save $92.64)	(Save $62.64)
	▶ Buy It Now	▶ Buy It Now	▶ Buy It Now

*Prices and terms subject to change without notice.

Save Time. Save Money. Make More Money. JOIN. TODAY!

CompleteLandlord.com Catalog (as of 12/31/08, Prices Subject to Change Without Notice.)

Newsletters

Landlord Profit Letter

The indispensable quarterly newsletter no landlord should be without, yours for just pennies a day!

Every month, important news breaks that can affect the world of landlording. Laws change. State rules and regulations change. And important real estate trends emerge that can affect your property, your tenants, your business — your future.

Where do you go for news, tips, updates, and detailed reports on the world of landlording? How do you know if you're following industry best practices? How can you save money ... avoid common pitfalls ... and maximize your rental returns?

The editorial team at CompleteLandlord.com has developed this newsletter to do what no other publication does: to go behind the scenes and bring all the news, ideas, tips, and statistics from the world of landlording together in one easy-to-read format. The CompleteLandlord.com team has more than 25 years of landlording, property investment, and rental management experience, and has helped hundreds of thousands of landlords save time and money since 1988.

Look what every issue of the Landlord Profit Letter delivers to you:

› How to Increase Profits — a different revenue generating idea each month, using examples provided by our seasoned and successful landlords!
› In the News — what's happening in laws, trends, markets, and headlines, and how they affect you. company (LLC) makes the most sense for you, your company, your employees, and your family.
› A Day in the Life of a Landlord — special regional accounts of landlord experiences, what they learned, and what they'll do differently next time.
› Time Saving Maintenance Repair Tips and Discounts — use just one of these tips and you have paid for your newsletter many times over!
› Landlord Landmines — the most common landlording pitfalls, and how to avoid them.
› Top 10 Lists — such as the Top 10 Ways to Save Money on Utility Bills ... Top 10 Ways to Get Your Tenants to Like You.
› Landlord/Tenant Laws — legal updates from our expert staff of attorneys.
› Weekly Polls — we ask and you answer ... listen to what your fellow landlords are doing across the nation.
› Vital Statistics — based on national and regional surveys of eviction rates, foreclosure rates, rent increases, and more.
› Questions and Answers — a review of the top concerns landlords are talking about in our Q&A Forum, along with useful advice.
› Plus Product Reviews, tips, cost-saving ideas, and more!

In landlording, you never know what you don't know. Learn how other landlords are boosting their cash flows in the landlording business or how selecting the wrong tenants can cost you thousands. You'll never know these secrets ... UNLESS you subscribe to the Landlord Profit Letter.

Knowledge isn't just power. Knowledge is money! Order the Landlord Profit Letter today!

The Landlord Profit Letter and CompleteLandlord.com are part of the family of brands from Minotaur Media, LLC. All CompleteLandlord.com and Minotaur products and services are reviewed and approved by attorneys, accountants fellow landlords, or industry experts.

Profit Letter Subscription
Price: $89.00
⊙ Order Now!

Books

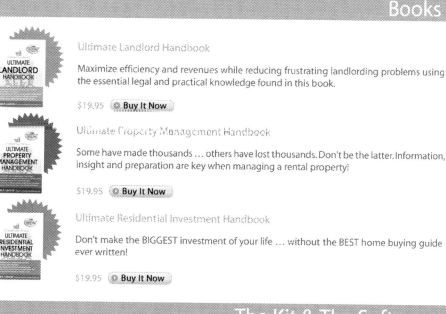

Ultimate Landlord Handbook

Maximize efficiency and revenues while reducing frustrating landlording problems using the essential legal and practical knowledge found in this book.

$19.95 **Buy It Now**

Ultimate Property Management Handbook

Some have made thousands … others have lost thousands. Don't be the latter. Information, insight and preparation are key when managing a rental property!

$19.95 **Buy It Now**

Ultimate Residential Investment Handbook

Don't make the BIGGEST investment of your life … without the BEST home buying guide ever written!

$19.95 **Buy It Now**

The Kit & The Software

Landlording Kit

Prepare yourself for higher profits and fewer headaches with step-by-step "real world" guidance on successful landlording. Includes important forms for your state. This landlord kit is essential for new or seasoned landlords.

$29.95 **Buy It Now**

Incorporation Kit

Protect your personal assets from operational risks and other business liabilities whether you're starting a new business or operating an existing one.

$49.95 **Buy It Now**

Attracting & Retaining Quality Tenants Kit

Discover the secrets smart landlords use to attract, screen, and choose quality tenants. Learn the easiest and most effective methods to find the best tenants.

$29.95 **Buy It Now**

Last Will & Testament Kit

Plan your estate responsibly and affordably with all the forms and instructions you need. Protect your loved ones, make your wishes known and award your assets as you desire with this kit.

$27.95 **Buy It Now**

Special Reports

Rental Property Management Secrets for Landlords

Rental Property Management Secrets for Landlords gives you tips from the pros on maximizing your income and minimizing your problems with the rental properties you own. You made a smart move becoming a landlord. Your portfolio of investment properties will ensure your financial future and a comfortable early retirement.

$19.95 ● **Buy It Now**

Tax Planning Secrets for Landlords

40+ page special report shows landlords how to maximize deductions on investment properties and save thousands of dollars a year at tax time! Now the editors and legal staff at CompleteLandlord.com have published a new Special Report, Tax Planning Secrets for Landlords, that can help you get every dime of tax savings you are entitled to as an investment property owner under current tax laws.

$19.95 ● **Buy It Now**

Eviction Secrets for Landlords

Evicting tenants is never fun. But whether it's the end of your problems —— or the start of much bigger problems —— depends on doing it right. When enough is enough —— know your rights, know the law and protect your property!

$19.95 ● **Buy It Now**

Complete Guide to Conduct Tenant Screenings

How to avoid troublemakers, late-payers and deadbeats by using "tried-and-true" screening methods for your rental properties. Looking for Trouble-free Tenants? Stop dreaming … And start screening … With the Complete Guide to Conduct Tenant Screening from CompleteLandlord.com!

$19.95 ● **Buy It Now**

How to Buy Foreclosure Property

Interested in investing in foreclosed properties? Want to avoid the major pitfalls that can cost you thousands? The real estate experts and editors at CompleteLandlord.com tell you all you need to know! When it comes to foreclosed properties, the right information and preparation can make all the difference between finding great deals … and losing your shirt. Our experts deliver the crucial up-to-the-minute information YOU need!

$19.95 ● **Buy It Now**

Understanding Rental Property 1031 Exchanges for Landlords

Are you a landlord or real estate investor who wants to sell your investment property and avoid capital gains tax? A 1031 Exchange might be the answer you are looking for. This report will help you meet your real estate goals and provide you with the education necessary to complete a successful 1031 transaction.

$19.95 ● **Buy It Now**

Memberships

Silver Premium Membership

Membership includes:

* Unlimited Access to Lease Creation Pro^{SM} Customizable State-Specific Leases and over 900+ State-Specific Forms and Letters
* CompleteLandlord.com Property Management Solution^{SM} (up to 2 rental units, included)
* 4 Issues of and Archive Access to Landlord Profit Letter^{SM}
* 1 Special Report covering a critical landlording topic
* 1 Topical Streaming Webinar/Audio Conference
* Unlimited Access to Content, Forms and Software Upgrades, Maintenance, Hosting, Storage, Multi-layer Security, and Rental Unit Scaleability

$9.97/mo - $97/yr   ◯ Buy It Now

Gold Premium Membership

Membership includes:

* Unlimited Access to Lease Creation Pro^{SM} Customizable State-Specific Leases and over 900+ State-Specific Forms and Letters
* CompleteLandlord.com Property Management Solution^{SM} (up to 10 rental units, included)
* 4 Issues of and Archive Access to Landlord Profit Letter^{SM}
* 3 Special Reports covering critical landlording topics
* 1 Tenant Screen and Background Check
* 1 Topical Streaming Webinar/Audio Conference
* Unlimited Access to Content, Forms and Software Upgrades, Maintenance, Hosting, Storage, Multi-layer Security, and Rental Unit Scaleability

$19.97/mo - $197/yr   ◯ Buy It Now

Platinum Premium Membership

Membership includes:

* Unlimited Access to Lease Creation Pro^{SM} Customizable State-Specific Leases and over 900+ State-Specific Forms and Letters
* CompleteLandlord.com Property Management Solution^{SM} (up to 50 rental units, included)
* 4 Issues of and Archive Access to Landlord Profit Letter^{SM}
* 5 Special Reports covering critical landlording topics
* 3 Tenant Screens and Background Checks
* 2 Topical Streaming Webinar/Audio Conference
* Unlimited Access to Content, Forms and Software Upgrades, Maintenance, Hosting, Storage, Multi-layer Security, and Rental Unit Scaleability

$29.97/mo - $297/yr   ◯ Buy It Now

News & Events

Tax Planning for Landlords: How to Save Thousands of Dollars On Your Taxes This Year – Webinar

Tax Planning for Landlords: How to Save Thousands of Dollars on Your Taxes This Year – Webinar

$99.00   **Buy It Now**

Series LLCs: How Landlords Can Maximize Their Asset Protection – Webinar

If you're a real estate investor, don't miss this CompleteLandlord.com Webinar where you'll learn how to reap the benefits of holding your real estate in a Series LLC.

$99.00   **Buy It Now**

The 10 Biggest Eviction Mistakes Landlords Make and How to Avoid Them – Webinar

If you've ever had to evict a tenant, you know what a nightmare it can be. If not, you should act now to prepare yourself -- before costly problems arise.

$99.00   **Buy It Now**

Tips

▸ Real Estate Tax Planning for Landlords
▸ Rental Property Management Ideas
▸ Tenant Screening for Landlords
▸ Problem Tenants and Handling Eviction
▸ Property Maintenance and Repair
▸ Rental Property Investment Strategies
▸ How to Avoid Clogged Drains
▸ Beginning the Eviction Process: Termination Notices
▸ Is a Property Management Company Right For You?
▸ Increase Your Bottom Line with Coin-Operated Laundry Machines
▸ Greening Your Rental Property
▸ How to Avoid High-Risk Tenants
▸ Handling Tenant Move-Outs
▸ Rent Collection Procedures
▸ Freshen Up Your Rental Property
▸ Beware: Eminent Domain and more

     Find these and other CompleteLandlord Products and Services at http://completelandlord.com/store.aspx

Order Form

Please provide us with some basic information to begin your free trial.

First Name* _____

Last Name* _____

Address* _____

Address 2 _____

City* _____

State* _____

Zip Code* _____

Phone* _____

Best Time to Call _____

No. of Properties _____

No. of Units _____

Desired Website Address** : http://_____. completelandlord.com

Company Name* _____

Primary Email Address* _____

I am a new customer _____

I am a returning customer and my password is _____

Tenant Screening

Irresponsible, destructive or criminal tenants can cost you thousands of dollars in property damage, missed rent, legal fees and court costs!

What secrets could your next applicant be hiding from you?

Your potential tenant won't let you know if he has a criminal record. She won't tell you if she's had prior evictions. But you'll find out — with a Tenant Screen from CompleteLandlord.com.

99% of the problems landlords face — from bounced checks to evictions — start with bad tenants. They don't respect you, they don't respect their lease, and they certainly don't respect your investment property.

But how can you know if the person who wants to rent your property is who he says he is? How can you know if she's responsible enough to make payments on time?

The answer is a Tenant Screen from CompleteLandlord.com

A CompleteLandlord.com Tenant Screen is the most advanced, most comprehensive way to screen prospective renters for your investment properties. Before you let prospects sign a lease, you'll run their identity through every relevant background check and search allowable by law, including:

> Credit Check
> Criminal Background Report
> Evictions Report
> Sex Offender List Search
> Terrorist List Search

Tenant Screen
Price: $24.95
Order Now!

The simple truth is, people will lie!

They'll forget, they'll falsify and they'll forge. Let a bad character into your rental property and, in the best case, you may lose a few hundred or thousand dollars … in the worst cases you may be liable for criminal activities that take place in property you own.

Don't let this happen. Get a Tenant Screen from CompleteLandlord.com today!

You wouldn't let a convicted felon into your home or allow a convicted sex offender to be around your children. Why would you let them into your rental property?

CompleteLandlord.com helps you be more profitable and productive in your landlording business. Landlording is stressful enough, even with great tenants. It's horrible with bad tenants.

What protected the landlords, their loved ones — and their expensive investment properties — can protect you, too. And the cost is far less than you might think — just $24.95 per Tenant Screen. A small price to pay for peace of mind!

Don't take chances with your property. The smiling face you see may not be who he or she claims to be! Protect your property and your security with a Tenant Screen from CompleteLandlord.com — the most comprehensive background check available without a private detective.

They may not tell you the whole truth. A Tenant Screen will. Order yours now!

Be Sure to Read and Benefit from the **Entire**
The CompleteLandlord.com Ultimate Landlord Series

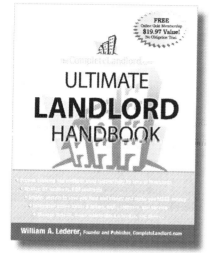

- Proven systems and methods used successfully by tens of thousands
- Written BY and FOR landlords
- Insider secrets to save you time and money
- Make MORE money
- Integrated online forms & letters, tools, software, and services
- Manage tenants, make maintenance a breeze, and more...
- Includes Free Online Gold Trial Membership

400+ pages $19.95/$23.95 CAN

- Insider Investment Strategies and Secrets from *the* Source
- Save Time & Money...Make *MORE* Money
- Find Properties that Will Increase Cash Flow and Work Best for *YOU*
- Streamline the Buy-Hold-Sell Process with Proven Online Tools
- Not a Get-Rich-Quick Guide--Get Rich the CompleteLandlord Way
- Includes Free Online Gold Trial Membership

350+ pages $19.95/$23.95 CAN

- 1 to 5,000 Rental Units - Know and Apply Industry "Best Practices"
- Avoid Legal Pitfalls & the Unexpected Managing Tenants, Vendors and Clients
- Sound Operating, Financial and Tax Advice from Experts
- Proven System and Methods Used Successfully by Tens of Thousands
- Integrated Online Forms & Letters, Tools, Software, and Services
- Includes Free Online Gold Trial Membership

250+ pages $19.95/$23.95 CAN